Container Gardening *for* California

Jennifer Beaver and Don Williamson

LONE
PINE

Lone Pine Publishing International

© 2009 by Lone Pine Publishing International Inc.
First printed in 2009   10 9 8 7 6 5 4 3 2 1
Printed in China

The Distributor: Lone Pine Publishing
1808 B Street, Suite 140
Auburn, WA USA 98001
Website: www.lonepinepublishing.com

Publisher's Cataloging-In-Publication Data
(Prepared by The Donohue Group, Inc.)

Beaver, Jennifer.
  Container gardening for California / Jennifer Beaver and Don Williamson.

  p. : col. ill. ; cm.

  Includes index.
  ISBN-13: 978-976-8200-52-5
  ISBN-10: 976-8200-41-3

1. Container gardening--California. I. Williamson, Don, 1962- II. Title.

SB418 .B42 2009
635.9/86/09794

Front cover photograph by Proven Winners

Every effort has been made to correctly identify photographers whose works are in this book. If we have erred, please let us know. All photos are by Laura Peters except: AASelection 171b; Sandra Bit 25a, 148b; Conard-Pyle Roses 181b; Tamara Eder 48a, 49, 55, 56, 67, 82b, 89, 110, 120, 122b, 128a&b, 134a, 138, 149b, 156b, 159, 174, 176, 182a&b, 186b, 192, 194, 209a; Jen Fafard 34; Derek Fell 78, 124b, 131, 180b; Erika Flatt 37, 77; Saxon Holt 54, 63, 80, 99, 218c; Janet Loughrey 123, 187; Heather Markham 132; Tim Matheson 36, 53, 58a, 68b, 83, 97, 98, 104b&c, 105, 106, 108a&b, 113, 114, 130, 137, 139, 149a, 156a&c, 162, 166b, 171a, 179, 191, 193a&b, 208; Kim O'Leary 82a, 118, 124a; Allison Penko 72, 93, 122a, 134b, 146a&b, 147, 154; Photos.com 204; Proven Winners 3a&c, 11, 17a&b, 19, 22, 24b, 45b, 50a, 51, 52, 57, 59, 61, 66, 71, 85, 87a, 88, 90, 94, 100a&b, 102a, 103, 115, 121, 125, 129, 140, 142, 151, 158, 161, 164, 168, 169, 172, 175, 177, 184, 185, 188, 189a, 197, 199, 200, 203b, 205, 207, 218b, 219a,c&d; Robert Ritchie 48b, 180a; Nanette Samol 26a,b&c, 29b, 38a&b, 39a,b&c, 40a,b,c&d, 43a, 47; Peter Thompstone 157; Vincent Woo 14, 15; Tim Wood 58b, 101a,b&c, 104a, 112, 145, 209b.

This book is not intended as a 'how-to' guide for eating garden plants. No plant or plant extract should be consumed unless you are certain of its identity and toxicity and of your potential for allergic reactions.

PC:*P14*

Table of Contents

Preface

Think you don't have a green thumb? Been disappointed with your growing results? This book will help you contain all your gardening problems.

Container gardening is the ultimate problem solver. Worried about conserving water in your general landscape? You can still grow your thirstier favorites in pots. No room in your condo for a vegetable garden? You can have a bountiful balcony by becoming a container-garden farmer.

Thanks to California's diverse climate, we can grow everything from evergreens to tropicals. We have cool, wet winters in the north, hot, dry summers in the mountains and deserts, and a mild and forgiving climate along the coast and southward. Regardless of what part of the state you call home, containers let you bend the rules of gardening for your area. With a little extra care, you can grow succulents in cool, rainy areas and bog plants in a desert. Use this book to help you let your garden and your imagination go to pots.

California is blessed with a huge variety of plant material and independent nurseries that grow and sell quality stock. Gardeners also have access to excellent, inexpensive potting soils. Container gardens are only as good as the soil that is placed into them, and high-quality packaged potting soils are available at every nursery and garden center. Good potting soil makes gardening in pots the easy answer to the most common growing problems.

Plants and potting soil are just two of the key ingredients for container gardening. The third component is the pot or container itself. The Pacific Ocean and the port cities along the coast bring an enticing selection of pottery to our area. Fired-clay pots from China, Thailand and Japan and rustic pots from Mexico arrive in vast lots from huge ships and quickly find their way into local nurseries and garden centers. Looking for something really distinctive? Local artisans can create one-of-a-kind vessels that will make your garden the talk of the neighborhood. Or, with an hour and a few dollars, you can transform an ordinary pot into something special using paint made just for plastic.

But why buy a pot at all? Communities in California are full of independent and creative people who can turn just about any receptacle into a container for growing plants—from recycled bathtubs to rusty colanders and metal tool boxes. These unique containers showcase the resourcefulness of our local people in award-winning home and show gardens.

Containers are the gardener's ultimate creative outlet. To inspire you, a team of garden writers has put together the images, planting suggestions and how-to information with the goal of giving container gardening a fresh twist. We want to get you growing and unleash your inner artist as well. You'll see vegetables mixed with flowers, formal urns with topiary, new plant varieties with old-fashioned favorites—combinations that you may have never considered happily growing together in pots.

People garden as a way to make their space more beautiful, to de-stress and to have fun. Gardening in containers makes it easier to achieve all these goals. Dig in!

The Plants at a Glance

Pictorial Guide in Alphabetical Order

African Daisy
p. 52

Agapanthus
p. 53

Aloe
p. 54

Angelonia
p. 55

Angel's Trumpet
p. 56

Arborvitae
p. 57

Argyranthemum
p. 59

Asparagus Fern
p. 60

Bacopa
p. 61

Basil
p. 62

Bay Laurel
p. 63

Begonia
p. 64

Bidens
p. 66

Black-Eyed Susan
p. 67

Black-Eyed Susan Vine
p. 69

Blood Grass
p. 70

Blue Fescue
p. 71

Blue Oat Grass
p. 72

Bougainvillea
p. 73

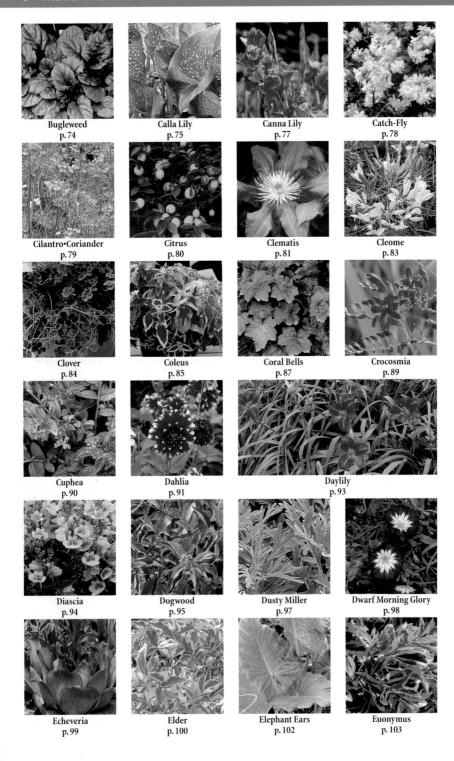

Bugleweed
p. 74

Calla Lily
p. 75

Canna Lily
p. 77

Catch-Fly
p. 78

Cilantro•Coriander
p. 79

Citrus
p. 80

Clematis
p. 81

Cleome
p. 83

Clover
p. 84

Coleus
p. 85

Coral Bells
p. 87

Crocosmia
p. 89

Cuphea
p. 90

Dahlia
p. 91

Daylily
p. 93

Diascia
p. 94

Dogwood
p. 95

Dusty Miller
p. 97

Dwarf Morning Glory
p. 98

Echeveria
p. 99

Elder
p. 100

Elephant Ears
p. 102

Euonymus
p. 103

Euphorbia p. 105	False Cypress p. 107	Fan Flower p. 109	Flowering Maple p. 110
Foamflower p. 111	Fothergilla p. 112	Fuchsia p. 113	Gaura p. 115
Geranium p. 116	Glory Bush p. 118	Golden Hakone Grass p. 119	Golden Marguerite p. 120
Hardy Geranium p. 121	Hebe p. 123		Hydrangea p. 129
Heliotrope p. 125	Hens and Chicks p. 126	Hosta p. 127	
Hyssop p. 131	Impatiens p. 132	Iris p. 133	Japanese Painted Fern p. 135

Jasmine
p. 137

Kalanchoe
p. 138

Lady's Mantle
p. 139

Lamium
p. 140

Lantana
p. 142

Lavender
p. 143

Licorice Plant
p. 144

Lilac
p. 145

Lilyturf
p. 147

Lobelia
p. 148

Lotus Vine
p. 150

Lungwort
p. 151

Lysimachia
p. 152

Million Bells
p. 157

Maidenhair Fern
p. 153

Mandevilla
p. 154

Maple
p. 155

Mondo Grass
p. 158

Monkey Flower
p. 159

Nasturtium
p. 160

Nemesia
p. 161

Nicotiana
p. 162

Oregano
p. 163

Oxalis
p. 164

Pansy
p. 165

Parsley
p. 167

Penstemon
p. 168

Perilla
p. 169

Petunia
p. 170

Phlox
p. 172

Phormium
p. 173

Piggyback Plant
p. 174

Plectranthus
p. 175

Poor Man's Orchid
p. 176

Purple Fountain Grass
p. 177

Rhododendron•Azalea
p. 179

Rose
p. 181

Rosemary
p. 183

Rush
p. 184

Salvia
p. 185

Scarlet Runner Bean
p. 187

Sedge
p. 188

Sedum
p. 190

Serviceberry
p. 191

Snapdragon
p. 192

Snow-in-Summer
p. 194

Spider Plant
p. 195

Spruce
p. 196

Swan River Daisy
p. 197

Sweet Alyssum
p. 198

Sweet Flag
p. 199

Sweet Potato Vine
p. 200

Thyme
p. 202

Tradescantia
p. 203

Tulip
p. 204

Verbena
p. 205

Vinca
p. 206

Weigela
p. 207

Yarrow
p. 208

Yew
p. 209

Yucca
p. 210

Introduction

People are passionate about container gardening. Well-stocked garden centers and creative propagators have made it one of the most exciting and fast-growing segments of the garden industry. Container gardening is almost irresistible because it offers something for everyone. Both practical and flexible, it is also the source of sensory delight and satisfaction.

Why is it so popular? Container gardening is suitable for every level of gardening expertise, demographic and landscape, even if that landscape is only a balcony. Almost all the same plants that grace conventional gardens can grow in containers. Gardeners use containers to create theme gardens, plant orchards and grow flowers, vegetables and fresh herbs. They transform small decks or patios into tropical retreats,

English cottage gardens or shaded woodlands using pots of different shapes and sizes filled with varied plant combinations to achieve a certain feel, look or environment. Even one large container can provide all the pleasure gardening has to offer.

Container gardening can help people with limited mobility gain easy access to their gardens. A garden with wide paths, raised beds and containers is ideal for able-bodied gardeners but even better if you require the extra space for accessibility and stability. A stable, wide edge of a raised bed offers seating at a comfortable height—a perfect solution if you cannot work for extended periods while standing.

Container gardening enhances conventional gardens and landscapes. Intermingle containers with in-ground plants to extend your possibilities. Containers expand the space available for growing plants. You can go vertical, attach containers to walls and shepherd's hooks, or place some gorgeous containers on your patio.

Containers let you leap over pesky limitations such as poor soil, too much shade or too little water. With a container, you control the environment. Even if the rest of your landscape is supposed to be drought tolerant, you can lavish carefully hoarded water on a selection of happily blooming containers. Got an invasive plant? Corral it in a container. And if an overabundance of shade is a problem, there's usually a small patch of sun somewhere than can host a potted geranium or other sun-lover.

Portability is another feature that makes containers popular. Move tender plants to areas where they are protected from the elements. Wheel sun and shade lovers around the landscape as the seasons change so they always get what they need.

Draw admiring glances toward features such as doorways, sidewalks, driveways and garden paths by positioning containers nearby as focal points. Strategically placed containers can also attract attention away from items or areas you would prefer to remain unnoticed. Celebrating a season or a holiday? Look to containers to put on the appropriate display. Containers can rescue dilapidated beds and borders left frowsy by finished bloomers or decimated by pests or disease, or that were simply not performing as desired.

Containers are great places to experiment with companion plants, which form a symbiotic relationship when planted together. For example, one plant may provide protection from pests while its companion provides essential nutrients. Some plants improve growing conditions for their companions by shading roots or suppressing weed growth.

Container gardening can save time and money. Many chores such as weeding, lawn mowing, digging and raking are reduced or eliminated. The use of automated watering systems or water-holding polymers and other materials, combined with slow-release fertilizers, can make your container garden very low-maintenance. A smaller, more contained garden area will also cost less than an average in-ground garden. After an initial investment in containers and a few tools and supplies, your annual costs will include only plants, fertilizer and growing media. As you gain experience, you'll learn how to further cut costs and reduce the overall amount of work involved.

Let your imagination run wild, and remember that mistakes are part of the learning process. Keep an open mind and have fun experimenting.

Vertical, Rooftop and Drought-tolerant Gardening

Vertical Gardening

Vertical gardening offers many advantages. You can maximize a limited space, such as a balcony or patio. You can block an ugly view or provide privacy. Vertical gardens also allow the disabled and elderly easier access for maintaining plants and enjoying the garden.

Vertical gardening is as easy to do in containers as it is in a regular garden. Containers can include raised beds, planter boxes, hanging baskets—anything sturdy and stable enough for the plants you intend to grow.

Vines and other natural climbers can be trained to grow up trellises, fences, arbors and walls, using space that would otherwise be empty. Vines employ various attachment methods. Some twine, others use tendrils, aerial rootlets or suction cups, and some require human intervention. Make sure that the container and climbing structure can handle the weight of the plant without tipping over and that it will not blow over in a strong wind. If you're putting a climber on the side of your house, remember to leave a 1–2" gap between the plant's support and your dwelling. This will reduce trapped moisture and other unpleasant side effects that can harm your home's exterior.

Hang baskets from any sturdy support, ranging from commercially available poles to house eaves to tree branches. Try raising and lowering them with a pulley system to simplify maintenance. A small block-and-tackle system will allow heavy containers to be raised and lowered with ease. A knot tied in the pulley rope will help prevent the container from hitting the ground if the rope slips out of your hands. Use a ladder to reach high baskets if a pulley system is not possible, and use a hose-end watering wand to reach up and into hanging baskets. Make it easy on yourself—hanging baskets dry out quickly!

Specialized containers include those with multiple openings, such as strawberry pots. A terracotta strawberry/herb planter has a large opening at the top and smaller openings around the sides. To irrigate these properly, when you plant the container insert a 1.5" diameter PVC pipe drilled with small holes from top to bottom. Water will drizzle out the length of the pipe to reach all the plants. Stackable containers also maximize available space. Growing walls are containers that have a vertical planting surface. One type of growing wall is a tall, flat, upright container that resembles a section of lattice fence with plants poking out of it. Another type is a wall constructed of custom-formed cinder blocks that provide planting pockets at regular intervals. A growing wall can stand alone or be incorporated as part of a building wall, fence or barrier. Also available are retaining wall blocks with pre-formed planting pockets in the design, so your whole retaining wall can be planted.

Vertical gardens can reduce or eliminate some pest problems. Hanging baskets prevent crawling pests from

reaching the plants. Also, the plants are more exposed to air, which reduces many diseases.

Vertical container gardens require the same type of maintenance as your regular container garden, except that the plants may need to be watered more frequently. A layer of mulch helps retain moisture, but try to position the plants within easy reach for maintenance. When planning your vertical container garden, determine if it will shade other plants (remember that the amount of shade will increase as the season progresses). If your plants flourish in the sun, place the climbing structure on their north side. Do the reverse for shade-loving plants. Also, face the plants into the direction of the prevailing wind so that it pushes the plants onto the structure.

Rooftop Gardening

Rooftop gardening is one of the latest trends in the horticultural arena. Rooftop gardens come in different forms, from a thick layer of soil over an impermeable membrane that covers most of the roof surface to a collection of various containers set on the roof. Why are they so popular? Lots of reasons. They attract fewer pests than ground-level containers because any pest that has to crawl or walk to find its host, such as a browsing deer, is out of luck. Vandalism and theft are practically eliminated as

well. Rooftop gardens in large urban centers provide respite for birds and butterflies that might otherwise lack adequate food and shelter.

Before tackling this type of garden, make sure your roof is sturdy enough to handle the weight of the pots, plants, soil and water. They are heavier than you think. Gardeners in areas that receive appreciable snow cover may need to remove their containers at the end of each growing season; the roof might not take the weight of the containers and snow combined. A structural engineer can determine how much weight your roof can hold.

A handy water source is essential; rooftop plants dry quickly in the wind and sun. A rain barrel will lessen the number of buckets you need to haul. Harness the power of water-holding polymers in potting soil and mulch to help keep the containers moist.

Rooftop gardens tend to be warmer and drier than ground-level gardens, which may extend the growing season. That's the good news. The bad news is that winds at rooftop level can be strong enough to break trees and shred herbaceous plants. Consider sturdy windbreaks to protect plants from strong winds and also to provide some shade from intense afternoon sun and some privacy from neighbors.

Some plants are better adapted to rooftop culture than others. Evergreens in containers are a possibility, though these will need extra protection in winter because wind and sun can quickly desiccate a plant. Heat-lovers such as hens and chicks and herbs are drought tolerant and make excellent roof dwellers. Remember, though, that even drought-tolerant plants need water to survive and look their best.

Drought-tolerant Gardening

In many areas of the state, people are turning to drought-tolerant gardening. Some do so because their municipalities have restricted water usage. Others enjoy the look, fragrance and relatively easy care of these plants.

Although the terms "drought-tolerant" and "California natives" are often used interchangeably, they can apply to different plants. Drought-tolerant plants are those that have relatively low water requirements. While many California natives meet that description, you don't need to confine your plant selections to California natives alone. Many other plants use water sparingly as well.

There are several approaches to container gardening with drought-tolerance

PROVEN WINNERS

in mind. You might choose from among the wide variety of water-thrifty sedums and hybrids. You could group plants with similar low-water requirements in a large container to maximize valuable moisture, or select a single large specimen for its own pot. Remember, however, that even drought-tolerant plants need water. Containers dry out more quickly than in-ground gardens and will require more water and excellent drainage.

Or you could go in the opposite direction and use your containers for thirsty plants and concentrate your water-conservation efforts on the in-ground landscape. Finding water to irrigate your container garden can be relatively easy, and you can still enjoy a variety of plants.

Throughout the plant directory, we've noted the plants that tolerate drought. In addition, you can often find useful information locally through your water department or community college.

Container Design

A well-designed container or group of containers can look beautiful with trailing plants cascading over the edges and colorful mounds of delicate flowers and interesting foliage filling the centers. Container gardening complements any setting—traditional, eclectic, contemporary or industrial. It appeals to gardeners who enjoy experimenting in their search for the ultimate combination as well as to those who follow the trends and switch from year to year.

The first step is choosing your plants. The second step is deciding how to combine them. Treat your containers like small flowerbeds, and apply the same principles of design as in your in-ground gardens. There are no hard and fast rules to container design, but the following suggestions will help you determine what will grow successfully and what will appeal to the eye.

As you embark on your design adventure, try useful online tools at popular propagators provenwinners.com and monrovia.com. Get ready to be inspired by the luscious plant combinations and to be enlightened by the wealth of information. These resources make it easier to choose plants that work well together.

Add interest by including a variety of flower shapes and at least three different foliage textures. Overall container garden designs look best with at least one strong, vertical element.

Group plants together that have the same needs, such as those that love water or tolerate drought or shade. This simplifies container care and can help prevent problems with pests and diseases.

When combining several different types of plants in one container, place the tallest ones in the middle or back. Place compact and trailing plants closer to the front or the edge of the container so that they are not lost visually. Robust trailing plants are good choices for the corners of square containers, where they have some extra room to spread. Careful planning allows for the best light to reach all plants, makes them all easy to see and enjoy and gives the containers an attractive, well-balanced appearance.

Another consideration is flowering time. Do you want the whole container blooming at once or do you crave a succession of blossoms? For continuously attractive containers, we recommend a 50-50 combination of blooming and foliage plants. Flower and foliage color are also important, as is the texture of the plants. Combining different features creates interest and contrast in your containers. Other design elements to consider include scale and proportion, shape, balance and repetition. Try before you buy by arranging your selections in a wagon or on the floor of the garden center.

You can use tall, sun-loving plants to provide shade for other plants. A trellis covered with tall, rapidly growing morning glories or scarlet runner beans will shade containers of impatiens or hostas.

Color

Color is often the first thing we notice in a garden. It is easy to make a dramatic statement with color in container gardens because they are confined and right in front of you.

Sometimes, knowing where to start is overwhelming. Take inspiration from home decorating and gardening magazines or anything else you see. Keep in mind that different colors have different effects on our senses. Cool colors, such as blue, purple and green, are soothing and can make small spaces seem bigger. Warm colors, such as red, orange and yellow, are more stimulating and appear to fill large spaces. White combines well with any color, and plants that bloom in white help to keep the garden from becoming a blurry, tangled mess.

Some principles used in interior design can also be used outdoors, especially in small spaces. Green combinations refresh while pinks and blues invoke romance. Fiery yellows, oranges and reds add liveliness and warmth to even the largest, most imposing spaces, and bronze, brown and neutral tones are contemporary and classy.

Two other tricks of the trade are color echoing and color harmonies. **Color echoing** is using one color, which can be of various hues and intensities, throughout the garden to produce unity and flow. This makes it easy for your eyes to flow from one part of the garden to the next without abrupt changes. Keep the color of your house, outbuildings and structures such as fences in mind when deciding what color or colors to use.

Color harmonies refer to different color combinations. A color wheel makes planning a snap. **Monochromatic designs** use a single color in varying hues and intensities as well as other colors very close on the wheel. For example, a monochromatic planting of yellow may include yellow-green without disturbing the harmony of the planting.

Analogous color designs use colors that are next to each other on the wheel, such as blues with violets and greens. These colors add a little more spice to a design while maintaining the same mood of the planting. **Complementary color designs** use colors that are opposite each other on the color wheel. These combinations make bold and dramatic plantings that attract attention.

Polychromatic color designs are some of the easiest designs to create because they most closely resemble the designs done by Mother Nature—a mixture of colors and textures seemingly tossed together in a haphazard manner.

The use of black, white and gray makes other colors really stand out, adds depth to small areas and plantings and helps tone down strong and complementary colors. Nearly black plants add mystery and intensity. White plants lighten the mood. If you spend time outside during the evening, consider an all-white container garden. You'll love the fragrance and luminosity of the plants.

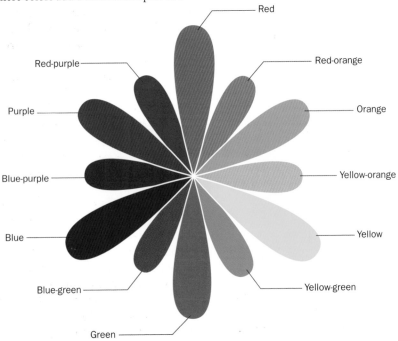

Red

Red-purple

Red-orange

Purple

Orange

Blue-purple

Yellow-orange

Blue

Yellow

Blue-green

Yellow-green

Green

Texture

Texture is an important consideration because different plant textures affect the perception of garden size and space. Some gardens have been designed solely on the basis of texture.

Foliage is the most important plant feature for achieving different textures. Large leaves are considered coarsely textured. Their visibility from a greater distance makes spaces seem smaller and more shaded. Small or finely divided leaves are considered finely textured and create a sense of greater space and light. Textures, colors and size of foliage can vary greatly, creating a myriad of combinations.

Integrating textural foliage into a container design encourages closer inspection. Flowers come and go, but a container garden planned with careful attention to foliage, using a mix of coarse, medium and fine textures, will always be interesting.

Scale and Proportion

The scale and proportion of plants should match the size of the containers. Large containers generally look best when they contain many plants, and small containers are best with a few plants. For container designs featuring a tall focal plant, the finished height should ideally be one to one-and-a-half times the height of the container. Exceptions might include large specimen plants, which demand their own containers or at most have a fringe of trailing plants, and which often exceed the suggested plant-to-container height ratio.

The scale and proportion of the containers and plants should complement their surroundings. Often one large,

The scale and proportion of your containers should match their surroundings.

well-planted container looks better in a small location than an array of little pots. Window boxes should match the style of the surrounding structure, and the plants within the window boxes should enhance the space both inside and outside the window. Too much height blocks sunlight from the house, but some height in the middle of the box can be a nice touch. Trailing plants look best when they don't touch the ground.

Shape

For variety, choose plants with different shapes to add drama and emotion or tranquility and peacefulness. Imagine the silhouette of a city skyline. Think how dull it would look if all the buildings were mundane square blocks, all the same size. Tall, structural plants are effective alone but also work as the main feature within a mixed arrangement.

PROVEN WINNERS

Rounded, billowy plants add bulk. Short, trailing or mat-forming plants soften the edges and add depth, effectively increasing the diameter of the container. Short, upright plants are great for filling open spots. Also consider the shapes of your containers and the way they look together. Strategic placement creates stunning results as one shape builds upon another.

Balance

To visualize the impact of balance, think of a scale where what is on one side must balance with what is on the other. In a design, balanced plantings are pleasing to the eye. **Symmetrical balance**, often used in formal gardens, occurs when one half mirrors the other. **Asymmetrical balance** is where the two sides are not the same but have the same visual effect. For example, a tall, narrow plant flanked by a mid-sized oval plant on one side and a shorter, wider plant on the other would be asymmetrically balanced. A radial planting has a central focal point with arms radiating out in all directions. Radial symmetry is achieved when all arms are balanced.

Repetition

Repeating colors or shapes at intervals throughout the garden helps tie the whole design together. Repetition is a design element that is fundamental to many of the great gardens of the world. Whether on a large or small scale, identical repeated plantings can emphasize or exaggerate perspective along a pathway, entrance or succession of steps. A row of identically planted pots can bring a sense of continuity to a space that seems chaotic and unbalanced, but it can also provide appeal to an empty space that begs for a simple focus. Placing a succession of large containers that stand above other in-ground plantings can create a stunning focal point.

Other Design Considerations

Grouping Containers

Design principles also apply to the grouping and placement of the containers. With careful positioning, a group of different containers can be arranged together for a greater impact. Remember to move the containers slightly away from each other as the plants mature to allow the plants to fill in and the sun to reach the leaves.

Containers often look best when placed in a triangular outline. They can be configured with a tall or large container in the middle with smaller pots on each side, or with a tall container on one end and successively smaller containers sloping down to the other end.

Formal placements often involve an **even** number of containers, such as a pair of square pots marking the front entrance of a house or two rows of containers forming an allée. Modern, eclectic and contemporary settings are best suited to repeated plantings with an **odd** number of containers as the focal point. A row of hanging plants looks best when all the containers are identical; however, the plantings do not need to be exactly the same. Cottage gardens, large rustic gardens with wild areas and other informal areas can benefit from a scattering of odd containers.

Adjusting pot height is another way to create a more luxurious display. Consider raising some of the containers on upturned pots, pot stands or shelves to offer additional interest.

Themes

Individual containers and groups of containers can follow any theme of your choosing—Mediterranean, native, tropical, cottage or whatever you fancy. A fragrance or aromatherapy garden full of herbs and scented flowers is perfect for seating areas and window boxes. Try planting an individual container with a single scent and move it into place to enhance a specific mood. Alternatively, one large container packed with a number of scents could delight loungers in nearby chairs. Container gardens lend themselves well to novelty themes, such as a salsa garden in which the plants make up most of the ingredients. One fun theme combines pots with painted faces with plants used to depict fanciful hair. Container gardening is also well suited for cameo gardens, small themed places tucked away from the main planting area.

Creative Design Tips

Remember that anything that can hold soil and provide drainage is a potential container for creative gardeners. There is no need to contain your enthusiasm when you get creative with these container ideas:

Desert-themed containers with cacti and succulents.

• Pot sedums and succulents in old leather shoes or boots. Nail cowboy boots to a wooden fence or hang a purse from a tree branch and pot it with trailing plants such as million bells.

• Metal wheelbarrows and wagons make great container gardens because they can be easily moved about for winter storage or to chase the sun. If metal containers are rusting out, line them with wire mesh and use rust preventive spray paint to restore them.

• Gardeners on the go might like old suitcases or footlockers to display potted plants. You can line old leather suitcases with plastic garbage bags, drill drainage holes and pot directly into the suitcase or metal footlocker.

• Need more space for more pots? Paint a ladder a bright color and place potted plants on the steps.

• Cracked and broken pots can still be put to good use. Lay broken pots on their sides half buried in the ground. Creeping plants such as petunias can grow from the opening, and it will

• Wine corks around the base of potted plants make a lightweight mulch and are especially suitable around Mediterranean herbs such as basil, oregano and thyme.

• Chipped or cracked china plates or brightly colored plastic plates can be set upright and half buried into container gardens. For a unified theme, use plates that match your regular outdoor dining set. For variety, choose bold or bright contrasting colors to provide a backdrop for blooming or trailing plants that spill over the container.

• Metal or stone remnants or architectural salvage can become the focal point of a large container garden. Imagine a slightly tilted stone pedestal or rusty metal bracket emerging from the center of a pot. Once the plants fill in around this accent, they'll have the "old world" look of a lost garden amidst the ruins.

• Mirrored gazing balls or glass orbs tucked into the soil around the plants will draw the eye to a container garden and help reflect the colors of the blooms.

appear that the pot has fallen over and is spilling out the blooms.

• A trio of pots in three different sizes can be stacked and planted for a tower of flowers. Place an upside-down plastic nursery pot in the bottom of the largest pot and balance the medium sized pot on top. Fill in with soil around the base to help support the medium-sized pot sitting inside the large pot. Repeat the process by placing the smallest pot inside the medium pot and using hanging plants around the sides. You'll have a pyramid of pots.

Adding Accents to Your Potted Gardens

Container gardens can contain more than just plants. Early in the season, there are often spaces between young plants. Add interesting accents, personality and color while you wait for the plants to fill in. Here are a few ideas.

• Polished stones or marbles add a bit of shine when used as mulch.

PROVEN WINNERS

Container Selection

Containers range from fancy pots and urns to wooden barrels, planters and window boxes, hanging baskets, wash-tubs and bathtubs, raised beds, galvanized metal buckets and even a pair of old boots. You can experiment with different pots to see what appeals most to you. Anything that is sturdy enough to handle the weight of the plant and potting mix and will not fall over can be used as a container.

Bigger is better. A large container is less susceptible to temperature fluctuations and requires less frequent watering. Large containers protect any bulbs, perennials, trees or shrubs you want to overwinter. Choose containers that are at least 12" in height and diameter. Smaller pots dry out very quickly, restrict the root area and reduce the plants' available resources. Deep-rooted plants need deeper pots.

Ensure that any container you use, regardless of the size, has adequate drainage. Drainage holes are either on the side of the container near the bottom, or on the bottom of the container. If your container does not have drainage holes, grab the appropriate drill bit and make some. Containers can be set on bricks or commercially available "pot feet" to help with the drainage. If you don't want to purchase pot feet, you can hide small tiles or chipped saucers under the pots to raise them off the ground just a bit, making sure you don't block the drainage holes.

Depending on where your container garden is, such as on a balcony, you may need to use drip trays or saucers. Saucers are most often made from clay or synthetic materials. Terracotta saucers retain moisture and may damage wood or painted surfaces. Saucers help conserve water, which is important in many parts of the state.

The drainage holes on the bottom of the pot will need to be covered with some material to prevent loss of potting mix. Use materials such as fine metal or

Unglazed terracotta pots (above) and glazed containers (right).

plastic mesh, newspaper, weed barrier, broken clay flowerpot pieces (crocs), coffee filters or cheesecloth. Many container gardeners will add a 1–2" layer of coarse gravel over the screen to help improve drainage, but this is not necessary because today's plant mixes drain very well. Using gravel, however, will help keep pots stable and will reduce the amount of planting mix needed in the container.

Light-colored containers are preferable, especially in sunny situations. They reflect light and will not heat up as much in the sun. This is especially important in spring when overly warm soil can stimulate early plant growth that could be damaged by inclement weather. Dark containers are ideal for design purposes because they provide a visual anchor like no other; just be cautious how you use them.

If you plan on moving your containers, especially the large, heavy ones, make it simpler by using wheels. Heavy-duty drip trays, saucers and basic platforms are now available with wheels that let you roll your containers around with relative ease. A locking mechanism will prevent unwieldy pots from rolling off on their own.

Materials

Container materials include clay, metal, wood, stone and synthetics such as plastic and fiberglass. Some materials are more appropriate for certain containers. Window boxes, for example, are usually made of wood or plastic. One reason is that weight is a critical factor. Another is that wood is traditionally used to create custom window boxes that blend in with the architecture. Raised beds are built from wood, brick or stone and can also be designed to flow with the building architecture and existing landscape. Hanging baskets may be wood, plastic or wire, with weight again being an important factor. A number of attractive stands are available that provide sturdy support for hanging baskets.

Clay

Clay pots come in two basic forms—glazed and unglazed—in many shapes and sizes. Clay pots can be heavy, even when they are empty. They are subject to environmental conditions and can be damaged by cold weather. They require special care, especially in areas that can freeze up fairly solidly in winter and areas that experience numerous freeze/thaw cycles.

Unglazed clay pots are often referred to as terracotta. Terracotta containers are somewhat porous, which lets plant roots breathe easily. Because porosity also allows quick moisture evaporatioron, terracotta pots require frequent watering. Terracotta holds heat into the night longer than wood, metal or synthetics. Terracotta containers come in different qualities, and you often get what you pay for. Pots from Italy and other Mediterranean countries are usually very good quality. Terracotta ages beautifully like no other container material. Within a few seasons, a combination of salts and organic growth will build on the walls of the pot, resulting in a lovely, natural patina. If this look is not for you, coat your terracotta pots with linseed oil to help remove the salt build-up and give a shiny patina.

Terracotta simply means "baked earth," referring to the kiln-firing process used in making the pots.

Glazed clay containers offer another way to incorporate color into the overall design scheme of your garden. Glazed containers are not porous, so they will need a few drainage holes on or near the bottom. Glazed pots also benefit from a plastic lining, which helps prevent cracking if moisture seeps in.

Wood is great for building window boxes.

Wood

Wooden containers are very adaptable and can be custom-built to fit into their surroundings. Wood offers more insulating value than clay, metal and stone, but it is susceptible to rot, so containers are often lined with plastic or coated with a non-toxic wood preservative. Some woods, such as cedar (*Thuja*), are relatively rot resistant. Do not use wood that has been treated with creosote or other toxic substances because it can emit compounds that can harm your plants. Wood is amiable to a variety of climates and can be used throughout our area. Make sure the containers are sturdy. If you have wooden barrels, make sure the hoops and handles are firmly attached. To ensure the longevity of your wooden containers, particularly at the joints and seams, protect them with wood stain or wood oils, both of which enhance the natural grain and prevent cracking.

Use linseed oil to protect wood from drying out.

Stone

Stone choices include terrazzo, concrete, reconstructed, refurbished and natural. Stone containers are available in a vast array of shapes, sizes, styles and colors. They are heavy and difficult to move, so plant them after they are set in their permanent location, unless they've been placed atop a strong platform or cart with wheels. Aggregate planters that mix stone with other materials offer a varied look. Carved stone pots can be very expensive, but they will add a level of elegance to any formal container garden. A large rock with a trough makes a wonderful place for tiny alpine plants but may need drainage holes drilled through the bottom.

You can accelerate the aging process on the exterior of stone containers by rubbing a fistful of fresh grass across the surface of the pot. The stain will quickly fade to brown. Brushing a thin layer of yogurt onto a pot's surface will encourage algae and lichens to grow, but a shady and moist location is necessary for the best result.

Metal

Metal containers may be made of tin, copper, bronze, iron, steel or lead and range in shape from simple buckets to fancy, ornate planters and urns. Metal pots absorb heat, and that can damage plants, so be considerate in your placement. To protect the container from contact with the soil, line it with plastic or simply insert a plant in a plastic pot. In addition, make sure your metal containers have adequate drainage holes. To protect the drainage holes from rust, apply a coat of anti-rust paint.

Use a soft cloth and window-cleaning spray to maintain the bright, reflective surfaces of your metal pots. Do not use abrasive pads or cleaners. Be careful not to splash water or potting mix onto polished metal; the splashes may leave white calcium deposits, but they can be removed with a soft cloth.

Wire is used to make cage-like frames such as hanging baskets, planters and ornate plant stands that can double as planters. Line them with sphagnum moss or some other suitable material before planting.

Stone trough planter (right); a large aggregate container (left).

Synthetic containers come in all shapes and sizes.

Synthetic

Plastic and fiberglass are the most commonly used synthetic container materials. These containers come in a huge range of shapes and sizes, from whimsical plastic ducks and teddy bears to newer fiberglass varieties that resemble good quality terracotta containers. All plant containers need drainage holes, so make sure that yours have them. Synthetic containers are durable, lightweight and easy to move, and most are good quality and inexpensive. Low quality plastic containers can deteriorate in the sunlight.

Synthetic containers are reliable in all climates and locations. Lightweight and movable, they are a good choice for apartment or condo balconies. You can easily remove potting-mix stains, dirty handprints and general muck from most synthetic materials by simply using a soft cloth and soapy water. For tougher stains, a scouring pad may be necessary, but test a small, hidden area first in case the pad damages the surface.

Spray paints made especially for plastic make it easy to renew or refresh synthetic pots. Using matte black spray paint on any synthetic container will give it the look of a cast iron pot.

A dark container in partial shade.

A full sun location.

Container Gardening Environment

Sunlight

Container placement determines the amount of sunlight received. Fortunately, many containers can be moved to accommodate the plant's needs. Available light is affected by the position of the sun depending on the time of day and year, as well as by nearby buildings, trees, fences and other structures. Knowing what light is available in your garden will help you determine where to place your containers.

Four levels of light may be present in your container garden: full sun, partial shade, light shade and full shade. Full sun locations, such as along south-facing walls, receive direct sun for at least six hours a day. Partial shade locations, such as east- or west-facing walls, receive direct morning or late-afternoon sun and shade for the rest of the day. Light shade locations, such as the ground under a small-leaved tree, receive shade for most or all of the day, but some sun filters through to ground level. Full shade locations, such as under a dense tree canopy, receive no direct sun.

Too much shade causes sun-loving plants to become tall and straggly and reduces flowering. Shade-loving plants may get scorched leaves, or even wilt and die, if they get too much sun. Many plants tolerate a range of light conditions.

California sunlight varies widely in its intensity. Plants that love full sun along the coast may fry at higher altitudes, so be sure to keep your plant zone and microclimate in mind. Reflective materials can amplify the sun's intensity. In addition, heat can become trapped and magnified between buildings, baking all but the most heat-tolerant plants. Conversely, a shaded, sheltered space that protects your heat-hating plants in the humid, hot summer may become a frost trap in winter, killing tender plants that should otherwise survive.

Exposure

Your garden is exposed to wind, heat, cold and rain, and some plants are better adapted than others to withstand these forces. Buildings, walls, fences, hills, hedges, trees and even tall perennials can reduce exposure.

Wind and heat are the most likely elements to damage your plants, and cold can affect the survival of perennials, trees and shrubs. The sun can be very intense, and heat can rise quickly on a sunny afternoon, so only use plants that tolerate or even thrive in hot weather in the hot spots in your garden. Plants can get dehydrated in windy locations, and strong winds can knock over tall, stiff-stemmed plants. Plants that do not require staking in a sheltered location may need support in one that is more exposed. Temper the effect of the wind with hedges or trees. A solid wall creates wind turbulence on the downwind side, but a looser structure, such as a hedge, breaks up the force and protects a larger area.

All hanging baskets are particularly exposed to wind and heat. Water can evaporate from all sides of a moss basket, and in hot or windy locations, moisture can be depleted very quickly. Watch for wilting, and water regularly. Wire baskets will hold up better in adverse conditions if you soak the moss or other liner with a wetting agent, and add some to the water when you first irrigate. Add water-holding polymers to the plant mix in hanging baskets.

Rain—too much or too heavy—can damage some plants. Most will recover, but some are slow to do so. Grow-covers—light fabric supported by wire—allow sun, air and moisture in and keep bugs, birds and wet weather out. For exposed sites, choose plants or varieties that are quick to recover from rain damage. Many small-flowered petunia varieties and new petunia cultivars recover well from the effects of heavy rain.

Hanging baskets are often very exposed to the environment.

Frost Dates and Hardiness Zones

All gardeners need to be aware of frost dates and hardiness zones. Last-frost and first-frost dates vary greatly from year to year and region to region. They can also vary considerably within each region. Consult your local garden center for more specific information. Many plants are hardy enough to survive winter outdoors in a large container, and many others grow to a mature size in a single season, given the right conditions.

Annuals are grouped into three categories based on cold-weather tolerance: hardy, half-hardy and tender. Hardy annuals tolerate low temperatures and even frost. They can be placed in containers early in the year and may continue to flower long into fall or even winter. Many hardy annuals can be seeded directly into containers before the last spring frost date. Half-hardy annuals tolerate a light frost but will be killed by a heavy one. These annuals can be planted around the last-frost date and will generally benefit from being started early from seed indoors, just like transplants from garden centers. Tender annuals have no frost tolerance at all and might suffer if the temperature drops to even just a few degrees above freezing. These plants are often started early indoors and are not planted in the garden until the last-frost date has passed and the ground has had a chance to warm up. Some have the advantage of tolerating hot summer temperatures.

In addition to the first- and last-frost date information, gardeners need to know their hardiness zone. The USDA has created a hardiness zone map based on average minimum winter temperatures and plant survival data. Many plants also have a maximum temperature threshold, above which they may die. California has a wide range of hardiness zones. Check the map to find yours.

Perennials, bulbs, trees and shrubs are given a hardiness zone designation, but don't feel intimidated or limited by this information. Mild or harsh winters, heavy or light snow cover, fall care and the overall health of your plants all influence their ability to survive through winter.

In addition, local garden topography creates microclimates, small areas more or less favorable for growing plants that are out of zone in the rest of your garden. Microclimates may be created, for example, in the shelter of a nearby building or a stand of evergreen trees, in a hollow or at the top of a windswept hill, or near a large body of water. Microclimates can raise the zone a notch and allow you the possibility of growing a plant that everyone says won't thrive in your particular area. Experimenting with plants that are borderline hardy is a challenging and fun part of container gardening.

Trees and stairwells can create a microclimate for your containers.

Hardiness Zones
(BASED ON AVERAGE ANNUAL MINIMUM TEMPERATURE)

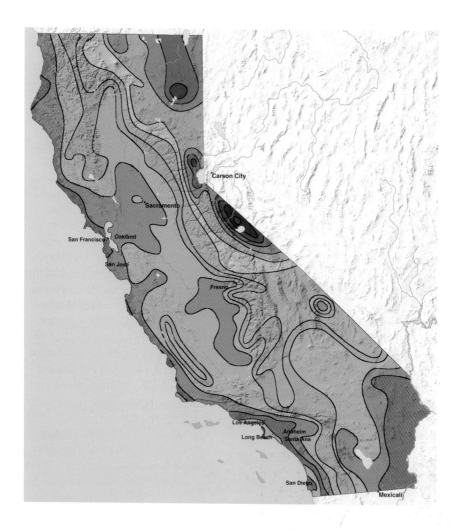

TEMPERATURE (°C)	ZONE	TEMPERATURE (°F)	TEMPERATURE (°C)	ZONE	TEMPERATURE (°F)
−23.4 to −26.1	5b	−10 to −15	−9.5 to −12.2	8a	15 to 10
−20.6 to −23.3	6a	−5 to −10	−6.7 to −9.4	8b	20 to 15
−17.8 to −20.5	6b	0 to −5	−3.9 to −6.6	9a	25 to 20
−15.0 to −17.7	7a	5 to 0	−1.2 to −3.8	9b	30 to 25
−12.3 to −15.0	7b	10 to 5	1.6 to −1.1	10a	35 to 30

Container Principles

Choosing Healthy Plants

The trip to the local garden center to choose plants is an important ritual in the world of many gardeners. These people often make one trip in spring and another in fall, a great time to plant in California. Other gardeners consider starting their own plants from seed one of the most rewarding aspects of gardening. Most gardeners purchase plants and grow them from seed; there are benefits to each method.

Perennials and shrubs for sale.

Purchasing is easiest and provides plants that are well established and often already in bloom, but it can get expensive. Starting seeds can be fun but impractical because it requires space, facilities and time. As well, some seeds require specific conditions difficult to achieve, or they have erratic germination rates. However, starting from seed is usually inexpensive and offers a greater selection of plants.

Get your plants, especially trees, shrubs and perennials, from a reputable source. These are likely to be with you for a while, so you want them to start out healthy. Plants grown locally will survive in your area better than those imported from elsewhere. Garden centers, mail-order catalogs, friends, family and neighbors are all great sources for plants and seeds. Some garden societies promote plant and seed exchanges. Many public gardens and gardening clubs have seeds of rare and unusual plants.

Staff at nurseries and garden centers should be able to answer your questions and make recommendations. Bring along an overhead sketch of the area where you intend to have your container garden and mark potential locations. Be sure to mark shaded areas, windy areas, garden and structure orientation (north, south, etc.) and so forth on the sketch so that they can help you choose appropriate plants. Take this book as well—you'll have information and photos at your fingertips.

The plants you buy are grown in a variety of containers. Most plants are

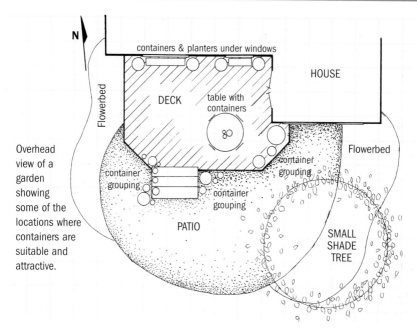

N

containers & planters under windows

HOUSE

Flowerbed

DECK

table with containers

Overhead view of a garden showing some of the locations where containers are suitable and attractive.

container grouping

container grouping

Flowerbed

container grouping

PATIO

SMALL SHADE TREE

sold in individual pots or divided cell-packs. Each type has advantages and disadvantages.

Plants in individual pots have been nurtured in the nursery and have plenty of space for root growth. They can be expensive and may be difficult to transport if you are purchasing many plants.

Cell-packs are often cheaper, hold several smaller plants per container and are easy to transport. However, because each cell is quite small, plants quickly become root-bound and should be planted as soon as possible after you buy them. Also consider that although smaller plants are more economical in the long run, they take longer to fill the container. For gardeners in a region with a short growing season, smaller plants may not be full and lush until late into the year.

For the best performance in your container, look for plants that haven't flowered. These are younger and less likely to be root-bound. Plants covered with an abundance of flowers or flower buds have already passed through a significant portion of their rooting stage, and although they will add instant color when planted, they will not perform at their best in the heat of summer, and their longevity can be compromised. If you choose to buy annuals or perennials already in bloom, pinch off the blooms and buds just prior to planting to encourage new root growth and a bigger show of flowers throughout the season.

Check for roots emerging from the holes at the bottom of the cells, or gently remove the plant from the container to look at the roots. An overabundance of roots means that the plant is too mature for the container, especially if the roots wrapped around the inside of the container resemble a thick web. Such plants are slow to establish once they are transplanted. Healthy roots will appear almost white. Avoid potted plants with very dark, spongy roots that can be pulled away with little effort.

A root-bound rootball.

Plants should be compact and have good color. Healthy leaves look firm and vibrant. Unhealthy leaves may be discolored, chewed or wilted. Tall, leggy plants have likely been deprived of light. Check carefully for diseases and insects, and do not buy a plant that has either unless you are willing to risk spreading such problems in your garden or can confidently deal with them before you bring the plant home.

Once you get your plants home, water them if they are dry. Plants growing in small containers may require watering more than once a day. Keep them in light shade until you plant them and remove any damaged growth.

Preparing Containers for Planting

Container Cleaning

Starting with clean containers minimizes soil-borne diseases and removes deposits from fertilizers and root compounds released by the plant. Clean new and used containers with mild soap and rinse well with water.

Terracotta pots require a different cleaning process. Soak them overnight or longer in a solution of nine parts water to one part bleach to make them easier to clean. Use a wire or stiff-bristle plastic brush to scrub the inside of the container, and scrape deposits off with a knife or scraping tool. Soak the scrubbed container in clean water for 15 minutes to remove the bleach and then rinse it with a quick spray. If you have glazed containers, make sure bleach will not damage the glaze.

Drainage

Most plants grown in containers require good drainage, unless you select ones that flourish in boggy conditions such as those found along streams or ponds. You may need to drill extra holes in containers that do not drain as quickly as needed; otherwise, your plants may drown. Another option is to set a planted pot with excellent drainage into a decorative container just as you would indoors. Make sure that water does not collect between the two pots; the rootball will become waterlogged and begin to rot. We recommend this arrangement only for small containers.

Choosing a Planting Mix

Many plants need soil that allows good drainage while still retaining sufficient moisture and nutrients. Commercially available container mixes do just that. In addition, they weigh less than garden soils and do not have soil-borne diseases or weed seeds. Do not use garden soil alone in containers because it drains poorly and tends to dry into a solid mass. A small amount of good garden soil mixed into the planting mix adds minerals and microorganisms and improves the nutrient-holding capacity, but it may also introduce soil-borne diseases. A variety of mixes are available, and you can make a selection based on your plants' requirements.

A selection of planting mixes.

High-quality compost should be an integral part of every container planting mix, and many commercial mixes now contain some percentage. Commercial mixes may also contain water-holding polymers.

Regular commercial planting mixes are mainly peat moss or coir fiber and may contain tree bark, vermiculite, perlite, dolomite lime, sterilized loam or clay, superphosphate for quick rooting and often some form of slow-release fertilizer. Coir fiber, made from the husks of coconuts, is more environmentally friendly than peat moss but can be harder to handle. Organic plant mixes come in different formulations depending on the manufacturer. They are mainly peat moss or coir fiber and may contain high-quality compost, composted leaf mold, bone meal, blood meal, humus, earthworm castings, bird or bat guano, glacial rock dust, dolomite lime, pulverized oyster shells, alfalfa meal, rock phosphate, greensand, kelp meal and beneficial mycorrhizal fungi.

These products are available in small and large bags and bales. You can also make your own from bulk ingredients to reduce your costs. For container plantings, we suggest using 40 percent sphagnum peat moss or coir, 40 percent high-quality compost, 10 percent garden loam and 10 percent washed and screened coarse, angular sand. You can add in high-phosphorous guano or bone meal for a root booster, or you can mix in a commercially formulated organic fertilizer. For plants that require alkaline soil, mix in dolomite lime or oyster shells to raise the pH. Add fertilizer products as instructed on the label for the volume of soil in your containers. A soil test is useful for determining what additions and adjustments your planting mix might need.

Reducing the Weight of Containers

Large containers full of plants and planting mix can be heavy. To reduce their weight, do not use gravel in the bottom and do not use planting mixes that contain soil or sand. If your large containers will hold only annuals, replace some of the planting mix in the bottom half with Styrofoam packing peanuts, broken Styrofoam packing pieces, well-crushed pieces of newspaper or shredded leaves, or flip over plastic pots and set them in place in the container before the planting mix is added. Perennials and shrubs, however, will probably need all the soil the container will hold for their roots.

Planting Containers

Generally, you can plant containers at the same time as an in-ground garden. Plant the largest specimens first and work down in size to the smallest—trees, then shrubs, bulbs, perennials and finally annuals.

To start, check your planned arrangement by placing the plants in position before removing them from the nursery pots. Fill your cleaned container with moistened planting mix until it is approximately 75 percent full. Once you've chosen where the plants are to go, begin working from the middle outward to the pot's edge. Install trellises, stakes or other needed supports. After removing the plants from the pots, gently tease the outside of the rootballs apart, or if the plant is root-bound, score the outer roots with a sharp knife to encourage the roots to spread out. Place the larger, central focal plants into the container first, followed by the smaller ones. Add more potting mix, as necessary, to surround the rootballs of the plants. Add the smallest and outer-edge plants last and top up the potting mix, allowing at

A selection of plants for a new container (top).
Place mesh screen over drainage holes (bottom).

least 2" from the top edge of the pot for watering and perhaps a layer of decorative mulch. Ensure the planting mix has no gaps or air pockets in between or under any of the plants by gently tapping the bottom of the pot on the ground or by slipping your hand into the potting mix to move the soil into gaps and pockets. Watering will also settle the potting mix without having to firm it down with your hands.

Water until the container is thoroughly soaked. Add more planting mix if it settles too much after the first soaking.

Don't plant too deeply or too shallowly. Use the depth at which the plants are already growing as a guide for how deeply they should be planted. You don't want exposed roots above soil level, but you also don't want to bury the crowns, which can lead to rot. If you're adding seeds to the mix, do so at this stage, planting at the depth recommended on the package.

The number of plants is a matter of preference, but overplanted containers look better than sparsely planted ones, except when you have specimen plants in their own containers. In containers, the space between plants can be less than what the plant's tag recommends. However, plants in a crowded container will compete for space, water, nutrients and light, so you will still need some soil between each plant to provide room for their roots to spread. Be aware that more plants in a container means more water and fertilizer.

Water plants regularly when they are first planted. Containers can dry out quickly, and plants need to become established before they can tolerate adverse conditions.

Fill the container with an appropriate amount of planting mix (above). Place potted plants in the container to check placement (center).

Remove plants from their pots and deal with any excess roots (below).

Tease out some of the roots on the bottom of the rootball. Make sure each plant has enough room. Water the freshly planted container immediately.

Some gardeners enjoy making detailed notes and planting diagrams to so they can repeat or avoid what they did in previous attempts.

Planting Trees and Specimen Plants

First make sure that the container is large enough to allow for root growth, and include enough planting mix to insulate the roots and crown from extreme climate conditions. Planting mixes for trees should have garden loam as part of the mix—it stabilizes the container and gives the tree something a little more solid to root into.

Most plants, especially trees, shrubs and perennials that you want to overwinter, should be planted in spring or early summer to give them enough time to establish before winter. Some gardeners prefer to keep hardier plants in containers for only one growing season, and then plant them in the ground later on. Others simply treat their container plants as annuals and don't overwinter them.

Container Garden Maintenance

Your container garden needs regular maintenance just like regular gardens, but on a reduced scale. The most important tasks are watering followed by feeding. Weeding, grooming, relieving soil compaction and repotting are other maintenance chores. You will need a few quality tools including a hand trowel, a hand cultivator, a watering can with a diffuser, a water meter and by-pass hand pruners.

Watering

Establish a water source before siting your container garden. You can use watering cans or buckets if you have a few containers. They come with a diffuser that makes the water flow in a gentle shower, which helps minimize soil compaction. For many containers, a hose with a watering wand is effective. Both methods take time, but you get to inspect your containers regularly. Water-holding polymers incorporated into the planting mix will act as a moisture reservoir, to reduce your watering time and cost.

Containers need to be watered more frequently than plants in the ground. The smaller the container, the more often the plants need watering. Containers, especially hanging baskets and terracotta pots, may need to be watered twice daily during hot, sunny and/or windy weather. To check if the container needs water, first feel the surface. If it is dry, poke your finger a couple of

inches into the planting mix. If it still feels dry, it is time to water. You can also lift the container off the ground a little, and if it feels light, it probably needs to be watered. Water until the entire planting mix is thoroughly soaked and water runs out of the drainage holes.

Even so, it can sometimes be difficult to determine if your containers are getting adequate water. Plants that get too much and those that get too little exhibit some of the same characteristics. In California, overwatering is one of the leading causes of plant death. To provide the best care, invest in a low-cost water meter.

If the soil in your container dries out, you will have to water several times to make sure water is absorbed throughout the planting medium. Smaller containers can be placed in a bucket of water until the surface of the planting mix feels moist.

Water until it drains freely out the drainage holes.

To save time, money and water, or if you plan to be away from your garden for an extended period, consider installing a drip irrigation system. Drip irrigation systems apply water in a slow, steady trickle, which takes somewhat longer than watering with a watering can or hose but still thoroughly soaks the containers. Drip irrigation reduces the amount of water lost to evaporation. Systems can be fully automated with timers and moisture sensors. Consult your local garden center or irrigation professionals for more information.

A thin layer of mulch will lower your watering requirements. To reduce evaporation from containers, group them together or place them in sheltered locations.

A special word about drought-tolerant plants. Regardless of what they're called, these plants still need water—and they need more water than they would if planted in the ground. Use the largest container possible and mulch, mulch, mulch to help them retain adequate moisture.

Feeding

Plants in containers have limited access to nutrients. If you use a good-quality planting mix that has compost and an organic or slow-release fertilizer, you may not need to add extra fertilizer for some time. However, fertilizer gives plants a boost during the growing season. Heavy feeders will definitely need additional supplements. Fertilizer comes in various forms including liquids, water-soluble powders, slow-release granules or pellets and bulk materials such as compost. Follow the package directions carefully. Excessive fertilizer can burn roots and kill plants or stimulate excessive plant growth that is susceptible to pest and disease problems.

Many plants will flower most profusely if they have access to enough nutrients. Some gardeners fertilize hanging baskets and container gardens every time they water, using a very diluted fertilizer to avoid root burn. Other plants, such as nasturtiums and many herbs, grow better without fertilizer and may produce few or no flowers when fertilized excessively.

Healthy soil allows plants to grow better. Organic fertilizers enhance the microorganism population in the planting mix, which in turn makes more nutrients available to the plants. Organic fertilizers don't work as quickly as many inorganic fertilizers, but they often don't leach out as quickly. They can be watered into planting mix or used as a foliar spray as often as weekly.

Organic fertilizers can be simple or complex formulations. They may include alfalfa pellets, well-composted animal manure, crab meal, coconut meal, corn gluten, kelp meal, sunflower

Organic amendments (left to right): moisture-holding granules, earthworm castings, glacial dust, mycorrhizae, bat guano, compost, bone meal and coir fibre.

meal, rock phosphate, humus, leaf mold, bone meal, blood meal, earthworm castings, bird or bat guano, dolomite lime, pulverized oyster shells, glacial rock dust, greensand and beneficial mycorrhizal fungi. Note that bone meal, fish emulsion and other odorous organic fertilizers may attract unwanted garden pests that can cause major destruction.

Containerized trees and shrubs benefit from removing some of the planting mix from the container every year and topping it up with fresh, good-quality compost.

Weeding

Weeding your containers is easiest when the weeds are small. Well-planted containers often suppress weeds by reducing the sunlight they need to thrive. Also, don't forget about the weeds that pop up around your containers.

Grooming

Good grooming helps keep your container plants healthy and neat, makes them flower more profusely and helps prevent many pest and disease problems. Grooming includes pinching, trimming, staking, deadheading, training vines and climbing plants, and pruning trees and shrubs.

Pinching refers to removing by hand or with scissors any straggly growth and the tips of leggy plants. Plants in cell-packs may develop tall and straggly growth; pinch it back when transplanting to encourage bushier growth. Remove any yellow or dying leaves. Pinch back excess growth from more robust plants if they are overwhelming their less vigorous container mates. Pinch off trailing stems before they touch the ground.

If annuals appear tired and withered by midsummer, use garden shears to trim them back a quarter to half of the plant growth to encourage a second bloom. Mounding or low-growing annuals, such as petunias, respond well to trimming. New growth will sprout, along with a second flush of flowers. Give the plants a light fertilizing after trimming.

Some plants have very tall growth and cannot be pinched or trimmed. Instead, remove the main shoot after it blooms, and side shoots may develop.

Pinching off a spent bloom.

Don't be afraid to trim any plant that is exceeding its boundaries.

Many annuals and perennials benefit from deadheading (removing faded flowers), which often helps prolong their bloom and prevents your containers from becoming a seed bank. Decaying flowers can harbor pests and diseases, so it is a good habit to pick them off. Some plants, such as impatiens and wax begonias, are self-cleaning or self-grooming, meaning that they drop their faded blossoms on their own. Seedheads left on some plants, such as ornamental grasses, provide winter interest.

Trees and shrubs need pruning to keep them healthy and in proportion to the container. Each tree or shrub has its own pruning requirements. Learn the best time to prune and how much can be safely removed to keep your containers in top shape. Research books, magazines and online for proper pruning techniques or attend a class at a college, university extension program or public garden.

Relieving Soil Compaction

Constant watering can compact your planting mix. When this happens, a hardened crust forms on the surface that does not allow water and air to penetrate. This crust can be easily broken up with a good hand cultivator. Replace the top layer of planting mix annually in spring.

Although dried-out plants have the opposite problem—not enough water—their issues are similar: water and nutrients can't get in. Fill a large pail with water and put in your dried out container. Hold it down until you see bubbles coming up and your container seems saturated. Let it recover in partial shade for several days.

Tall plants may require staking. Tie plants loosely to tall, thin stakes with soft ties that won't cut into the plant. Narrow ties are less visible. Stake bushy plants with twiggy branches. Insert the twigs into the planting mix near the plant when it is small, and as the plant grows it will hide them. A careful selection of twiggy branches can add another attractive dimension to your containers.

Vines in containers can be used as trailers or trained to climb up a trellis, netting or other structure. This structure is either inserted into the container, or the container is placed near the structure. Vines with tendrils climb easiest on small-diameter structures such as cage-like trellises or netting that are small enough for tendrils to wrap around easily. Other climbers will need to be woven through or tied to their structures. Do not be afraid to clip off any rampant or out-of-bounds growth.

Repotting Plants

Trees, shrubs and perennials can stay in containers for years with proper care and maintenance. At some point, however, you'll need to divide your perennials and root prune or repot your trees and shrubs. Perennials need dividing when flowering has diminished, when the plant loses vigor, when the center of the plant has died out or when the plant encroaches on the other plants in the container. Perennial divisions should be replanted as soon as possible after being split up. Spread divisions into other containers, share them with friends or compost them.

Trees and shrubs that need repotting will also appear less vigorous and have reduced flowering. If repotting, the rule of thumb for choosing new containers is to use the next larger size. Trees and shrubs will require containers only a couple of inches wider and deeper than their current pots, and they will need some root pruning. Using oversize containers can cause watering problems.

Tree and shrub containers can be heavy, and you may need help to tip the container over. Wrap the branches in a blanket to prevent damage before you do so. Gently remove the plant and shake out some of the old planting mix. Tease out the larger roots that are encircling the container or growing in toward the center of the root mass and cut them off where they would have just touched the edges of the previous container. When tree roots are pruned or damaged, the plant responds by reducing its top growth. Allow the plants to adjust naturally; wait and then prune off the dead branches when they become visible rather than pruning immediately. Replant the tree or shrub into its new

Learn proper pruning techniques before trimming trees and shrubs.

PROVEN WINNERS

home with fresh planting mix, ensuring that it is firmly settled with no air pockets.

Protecting Containers and Plants

Insulating Containers

Some plants prefer a cool, moist root environment during the heat of summer and some plants need extra protection from the effects of winter. Containers can be insulated in similar fashion for both situations. Some materials are better insulators than others. Rot-resistant wood such as cedar makes an attractive container that offers protection from excessive heating and cooling. Other containers may need help keeping the roots cool. One container placed into another with a minimum of 1" of space between them for insulating material such as moistened vermiculite, sawdust or Styrofoam packing peanuts is effective. The inside of a container may be lined with stiff foam insulation for straight-sided containers or with a couple of layers of carpet underlay for curved-sided containers. Coastal gardeners, because of the mild climate, can use a couple of overlapping layers of bubble wrap.

Protecting Containers from Frost Damage

Clay containers are subject to frost damage. Any water that has been absorbed by the container will expand as it freezes, causing cracks and chips. Avoid containers with narrow openings. When moist soil in the container is subjected to freezing temperatures it will expand, which can crack even the most sturdy clay or stone container. An opening that is equal to or larger than the rest of the container will allow freezing soil to expand up rather than out.

Containers with small openings might not allow freezing soil to expand.

Protecting Plants from Frost Damage

Protecting plants from frost is relatively simple. Cover them overnight with sheets, towels, burlap, row covers or even cardboard boxes. Don't use plastic because it doesn't retain heat and won't provide any insulation. Or move your containers to a frost-free area, such as a garage, garden shed or greenhouse.

Tender plants may have to be moved indoors in winter. They should be brought into the shelter of a greenhouse or the sunniest, warmest location in your house before the first frosts. Most tender plants can be treated as houseplants. If don't have space to overwinter large plants indoors, take cuttings in late summer and grow them for the following spring.

Grow tender plants in partial shade outdoors so that the plants will be accustomed to the lower light levels when brought inside for winter.

Protecting Plants from Heat Damage

In areas where summers are hot or even where the weather is temperate all year round, plants may suffer on scorching days. If dry, hot Santa Ana winds are forecast, provide extra water and consider wheeling top-heavy containers to a protected area so they don't blow over. Check your containers every day, and if the flowers or foliage look excessively wilted or crisp, move them to partial shade or rig up a temporary bit of shade using a garden umbrella or shade cloth.

Preparing for Winter

Storing Containers

Containers that will be emptied at the end of the growing season can be cleaned and moved to a suitable storage spot. Containers that can't be moved and have no plants can be emptied of planting mix and cleaned. Ensure all containers are in good condition, and if needed, repair them during winter. In areas that experience freezing temperatures, clay containers, especially decorative glazed containers, should be emptied and stored indoors.

Overwintering Hardy Trees, Shrubs and Perennials

Hardy trees, shrubs and perennials that you intend to overwinter will survive better if the plants are allowed to harden off as winter approaches. Reduce the amount of water and fertilizer the plants receive through late summer and fall, which signals the plants to prepare for the coming cold weather.

Planting mix can freeze solid when the temperature drops below 32° F. Plants continue to use water throughout winter, and even hardy plants can be killed because a frozen planting mix does not allow plants to take up moisture. The chances of plants surviving winter improve if containers have a large volume of planting mix. Water dry containers as soon as the planting mix thaws.

Overwintering Tender Rhizomes, Bulbs, Corms and Tubers

Dig up perennials that grow from tender rhizomes, bulbs, corms or tubers in fall after the top growth dies back. Shake the loose dirt from the roots and let them dry in a cool, dark place. Once dry, the rest of the soil should brush away. You can dust these modified underground stems with an antifungal powder, such as garden sulfur (found at garden centers), before storing them in moist peat moss or coarse sawdust. Keep them in a cool, dark, dry place that doesn't freeze. Check on them once a month, and lightly spray the storage medium with water if they appear very dry. If they start to sprout, pot them and keep them in moist soil in a bright window. They should be potted by late winter or early spring so that they will be ready for the outdoors. Some gardeners leave the tubers, etc., in the containers and store the whole containers inside over winter.

Pests and Diseases

Your container garden may experience attacks from pests and diseases. It's not traumatic because there are many ways of dealing with any problems that arise. Don't worry about soil-borne pests and diseases; they are almost non-existent in container gardens, especially when using soil-less planting mixes.

Containers often contain a mixture of different plant species. Many insects and diseases attack only one species of plant, so mixed containers make it difficult for pests and diseases to find their preferred hosts and establish a population.

Because annuals are planted each spring and different species are often grown each year, pests may have trouble

Aphids.

Powdery mildew.

finding their favorite targets. On the other hand, if you grow a lot of one particular annual species, any problems that do set in over summer may attack all the plants.

Perennials, trees and shrubs are both an asset and a liability when it comes to pests and diseases. These plants are in the same container for a number of years, and any problems that do develop can become permanent. Yet, if allowed, beneficial insects, birds and other pest-devouring organisms can also develop permanent populations.

Integrated Pest (or Plant) Management (IPM) is a moderate approach for dealing with pests and diseases. The goal of IPM is to reduce pest problems to levels of damage acceptable to you. Attempting to totally eradicate pests is futile. Consider whether a pest's damage is localized or covers the entire plant. Will the damage kill the plant, or is it only affecting the outward appearance? Can the pest be controlled without chemicals?

IPM requires learning about your plants and the conditions they need for healthy growth. Some plant problems arise from poor maintenance practices. For example, overwatering saps plants of energy and can cause yellowing of the plant from the bottom up.

By learning about the characteristics, habits and controls for pests that may affect your plants, you'll have a healthier and more satisfying garden. Keep records of pest damage because your observations can reveal patterns useful in spotting recurring problems and in planning your maintenance regime.

Prevention and Control

The best defense is to prevent pests and diseases from attacking in the first place by providing the conditions necessary for healthy plant growth. Healthy plants are able to fend for themselves and can sustain some damage. Stressed or weakened plants are more subject to attack. Begin by choosing pest-resistant plants. Keep your planting mix healthy by using plenty of good-quality compost. Spray your plant's foliage with high-quality, fungally dominated compost tea or fish emulsion, which acts as a foliar feed and also prevents fungal diseases.

Other cultural practices include providing enough space so that the plants have good air circulation and are not stressed from competing for available resources. Remove plants that are decimated by pests and dispose of diseased foliage and branches. Keep your gardening tools clean and tidy up fallen leaves and dead plant matter in and around your containers at the end of every growing season.

Physical controls are generally used to combat insect and mammal problems. Picking insects off by hand is one example and is easy with large, slow insects. You can squish or rub off colonies of insects such as aphids with your fingers. Other physical controls include traps, barriers, scarecrows and natural repellents that make a plant taste or smell bad to pests. Garden centers offer a wide array of such devices. Physical control of diseases usually involves removing the infected plant or parts of the plant to keep the problem from spreading.

Biological controls make use of populations of natural predators. Birds, spiders and many insects help keep pest populations at a manageable level.

Adult ladybird beetle.

Encourage these creatures to take up permanent residence in or near your garden, even though it may be difficult on balcony and rooftop gardens. Bird baths and feeders attract birds, which feed on a wide variety of insect pests. Many beneficial insects are already living in or near your garden, and you can encourage them to stay and multiply by planting appropriate food sources. Many eat nectar from flowers.

Chemical controls should be used only as a last resort. Pesticides can be either organic or synthetic. If you have tried the other suggested methods and still wish to take further action, try to use organic types, which are available at most garden centers.

Chemical or organic pesticides may also kill the beneficial insects you have been trying to attract. Many people think that because a pesticide is organic, they can use however much they want. An organic spray kills because it contains a lethal toxin. NEVER overuse any pesticide. When using pesticides, follow the manufacturer's instructions carefully and apply in the recommended amounts only to the pests listed on the label. A large amount of pesticide is not any more effective in controlling pests than the recommended amount.

PROVEN WINNERS

About this Guide

This book showcases 125 plants suitable for container gardening in California. The plants are organized alphabetically by their most familiar common names. Scientific or botanical names appear in italics after the primary reference, and additional common names, if they exist, are listed with the features of each entry. This system enables those who are familiar with only the common name of a plant to find that plant easily in the book. However, we encourage you to learn the botanical names. Common names are sometimes shared by several different plants, and they can change from region to region. Only the botanical name defines the specific plant everywhere on the planet.

The illustrated **Plants at a Glance** section at the beginning of the book allows you to quickly familiarize yourself with the different plants, and it will help you find a plant if you're unsure of its name.

Clearly indicated within each entry are the plant's height and spread ranges, outstanding features and hardiness zone(s). At the back of the book, you will find a **Quick Reference Chart** that summarizes different features and requirements of the plants; this chart is handy when you're planning what is best for your container garden designs.

Each entry gives clear instructions for planting and growing the plants in a container garden and recommends many of our favorite selections. Note: if height and spread ranges or hardiness zones are not given for each recommended plant, assume these values are the same as the ranges given with the features of each entry. If unsure, check with your local garden center experts when making your selections.

Be creative and have fun!

Plant Directory

African Daisy

Osteospermum

O. SOPRANO LIGHT PURPLE from the Proven Winners Selection SOPRANO SERIES

African daisies, with their unique colors, really stand out in a mixed container.

Growing

African daisies grow best in **full sun**. The potting mix should be **light, moist** and **well drained**. The plants are sensitive to overwatering but favor consistently moist soil. Fertilize every two weeks with half-strength fertilizer. Deadhead to encourage new growth and more flowers. Pinch back young plants to encourage bushiness.

Tips

African daisies mix well with other annuals such as petunia, verbena and sweet alyssum or with other daisy-like flowers for a daisy-themed container. African daisy blooms best during cool weather and will brighten up your containers in early spring and in fall when other plants start to fade. These cheerful blooms also attract bees and butterflies. Flowers open only in sunlight.

Recommended

O. ecklonis can grow upright to almost prostrate. The species is almost never grown in favor of its cultivars. **'Passion Mix'** includes heat-tolerant plants with pink, rose, purple or white flowers with deep blue centers and was an All-America Selections winner in 1999. **Springstar Series** loves heat but tolerates temperatures down to 28° F and comes in white and deep pink. **Starwhirls Series** has unique, spoon-shaped petals.

O. **Soprano Series** includes robust, upright but compact plants that have regular or spoon-shaped petals in white and shades of purple. Try **'Compact Purple'** in containers.

O. **Sunny Series** is larger and more upright than Symphony with an extensive color range and both regular and spoon-shaped petals.

O. **Symphony Series** has mound-forming, heat-tolerant plants that flower well throughout summer in yellow, orange, peach and white.

Features: white, peach, orange, yellow, pink, lavender or purple flowers, often with darker centers **Height:** 12–20" **Spread:** 10–20" **Hardiness:** perennial or subshrub grown as an annual

Agapanthus

Agapanthus

Even when not in bloom, agapanthus contributes clumps of bright green foliage to mixed containers, providing a lush background for companions with lots of flowers but sparse foliage or for taller plants with leggy lower limbs.

Growing

Agapanthus grows well in **full sun, partial shade** or **light shade**. Provide protection from the hottest afternoon sun. The potting mix should be **moist** and **well drained**. Roots may rot in poorly drained containers. Fertilize weekly during the growing season with half-strength fertilizer.

These hardy plants withstand temperature fluctuations and stay evergreen until about 25° F. Move them to a sheltered location during frosty weather.

Tips

Agapanthus makes an excellent filler plant. The strap-like leaves are bright green, and the rounded or pendulous clusters of flowers atop long, straight stems make excellent companions to flowering shrubs and large, shrub-like perennials. Yellow daylilies are a favorite companion plant.

Recommended

A. orientalis is evergreen and sports broad, arching leaves in big clumps. It is the most commonly planted.

Many hybrids and cultivars are available. **'Ellamae'** and **'Storm Cloud'** have deep blue flowers. White varieties include **'Queen Anne'** and **'Rancho White.'** Dwarf varieties include the popular **'Peter Pan,'** available in white, pale lavender and deep purple, and the blue **'Tinkerbell,'** which has attractive light cream and green variegated foliage.

A. campanulatus hybrid

Slugs and snails love agapanthus, so be vigilant in your pest patrol.

Also called: lily-of-the-Nile **Features:** clump-forming perennial; bright green, strap-like leaves; purple, blue or white, mid- to late-summer flowers **Height:** 12–36" **Spread:** 12–18" **Hardiness:** zones 7–10

Aloe
Aloe

A. barbadensis

Grown for its attractive long, pointed, fleshy leaves, aloe is a slow-growing succulent that does well in heat. Leaves may be green or banded with bright colors. Some aloes bloom monthly.

Growing
Aloe grows well in **full sun to full shade**, depending on the variety. Aloe's shallow root system means that the width of the container is more important that the depth. Use a **well-drained** potting mix with sand, perlite or pumice. Let the soil dry completely between waterings. Shelter containers or bring them inside during cold weather.

Tips
Drought-tolerant aloe is a beautiful long-lasting plant for a succulent container garden. It is an outstanding filler that looks good in the middle of a container. Favorite companion plants include sedum and kalanchoe.

Recommended
A. barbadensis (aloe vera) is an upright plant with medicinal value. Slit the fleshy leaves and apply the interior gel to burns and cuts, but do not ingest it.

A. gastrolea 'Midnight' from Proven Winners is a dark, dramatic aloe named to *Garden Design*'s Way Hot 100 list for 2008.

A. hybrids 'Fire Ranch,' with its spikes of red, orange, and yellow flowers, and 'Grassy Lassie,' with narrow, grass-like leaves that turn bronze in the sun, are Proven Winners varieties suitable for cooler areas to zone 7.

A. nobilis has dark green leaves with small, hooked teeth and grows in small rosettes.

Features: clump-forming habit; fleshy, solid or variegated foliage and occasional flowers
Height: 8–36" **Spread:** 12–24"
Hardiness: drought-tolerant annual grown as a perennial in warmer areas

Angelonia
Angelonia

A. angustifolia 'Blue Pacific'

This snapdragon look-alike provides a welcome vertical accent in summer containers and also makes a long-lasting cut flower. It's a favorite for cottage gardens.

Growing

Plant in **full sun** with **moist, well-drained** potting mix. Once established, angelonia is somewhat drought tolerant. Mulch to retain soil moisture. Angelonia can take heat and sun and will continue blooming when other plants have given up. The tall spikes of orchid-shaped flowers do not require staking and have a grape scent. It's hardy to 30° F.

Tips

These versatile plants mix well with a variety of companions including nemesia, coral bells, diascia, euphorbia and petunia.

Recommended

A. angustifolia features the **Angelface Series** from Proven Winners, which includes favorites **'Blue,'** a darker version, and **'Wedgwood,'** an unusual mid-range blue, and the **Angelmist Series**, which has lush blossoms in stripes and solids in white, pink, purple and lavender.

Also called: summer snapdragon
Features: upright spires with green foliage
Height: 18–25" **Spread:** 12–14"
Hardiness: annual

Angel's Trumpet
Brugmansia, Datura

All angel's trumpets add an exotic accent to the garden with their elegant, trumpet-shaped flowers.

Growing
Angel's trumpet grows best in **full sun** along the coast with afternoon shade in hotter areas. Shelter angel's trumpet from wind. The potting mix should be **moist** and **well drained**. Fertilize every two weeks with quarter- to half-strength fertilizer. Angel's trumpet is frost-tender, but *B.* x *candida* can be overwintered in a bright, cool room indoors.

Tips
Angel's trumpet flowers tend to open and be most fragrant at night. Place containers where you will enjoy them in the evening—near a patio, on a balcony or on a deck. They make excellent companions for other annuals.

Recommended
B. x *candida* (*B. aurea* x *B. versicolor*) is a large, woody plant that can grow up to 10' tall in a container and can be pruned to keep it smaller. It bears fragrant, white flowers that often open only on summer evenings. Many cultivars are available.

B. versicolor bears flowers in white or peach. **'Charles Grimaldi'** is a woody hybrid with large, funnel-shaped, lemon yellow flowers. It grows up to 10' tall.

D. metel is an annual plant that easily self-seeds. It grows 3–4' tall and wide and produces white flowers in summer.

D. metel with petunias and impatiens

Avoid using these highly poisonous plants in places children frequent.

Also called: datura, trumpet flower
Features: bushy habit; white, peach, yellow or purple, trumpet-shaped flowers **Height:** 2–10' **Spread:** 2–4' **Hardiness:** tender annual; woody shrub grown as an annual

Arborvitae

Thuja

T. plicata SPRING GROVE, a Proven Winners Color Choice Selection

These beautiful evergreens, with their soft foliage that won't poke you in close quarters, have dozens of dwarf cultivars that can last for several years in a big enough container. They provide a long-lasting, hard-to-find vertical element for large containers in cooler regions.

Growing

Arborvitae grows well in **full sun, partial shade** or **light shade** in a **sheltered** location. The potting mix should be **moist** and **well drained**. Keep plants well watered. Fertilize with a weak fertilizer no more than monthly in spring and early summer. Overwinter outdoors in a location out of strong winds and bright sun. Both can dry out the foliage and kill the plant.

Also called: cedar **Features:** evergreen shrub or small tree **Height:** 1–10' **Spread:** 1–5' **Hardiness:** zones 3–8

T. occidentalis cultivar (above)
T. occidentalis 'Danica' (below)

Tips

Arborvitae is popular for use as a screening plant on decks and patios. It can be grown alone or combined with flowering perennials and annuals. The larger the container the better because this woody plant consumes a lot of water.

Recommended

T. occidentalis (eastern white cedar) is a large, pyramidal tree with scale-like, evergreen needles. Many smaller and dwarf cultivars suitable for containers are available. **'Aurea Nana'** is a compact version with a globe shape and golden foliage that turns bronze in winter. It grows up to 6' tall and 3–5' wide in zones 6–9. **'Danica'** is a dwarf globe form growing to about 18" tall and wide with bright emerald green foliage. **'Emerald'** is narrow and upright and is considered one of the hardiest cultivars, more so if it doesn't dry out in winter. It grows about 10' tall and 36" wide before it needs transplanting to a garden. **'Teddy'** is a dwarf, rounded to oval plant, 12–18" tall and 24" wide, with fine, feathery, blue-green foliage that tinges bronze in winter.

T. plicata (western red cedar) has a few dwarf cultivars small enough for containers. The species and its cultivars are hardy only to zone 5. **'Cuprea'** is a low, mound-forming cultivar with bright yellow-tipped, bronzy green foliage. It grows about 36" tall and wide. **'Pygmaea'** has dark, blue-tinged foliage and grows 24–36" tall and 12–24" wide. **'Stoneham Gold'** grows about 6' tall and 36" wide. New growth emerges bright yellow and matures to dark green. **'Whipcord'** has long, pendulous, rope-like foliage that gives the plant a mop-like appearance. It grows about 36" tall and spreads about 30".

Argyranthemum

Argyranthemum

The daisy-like flowers seem to suit almost any setting.

Growing

Argyranthemums do well in **full sun** or **partial shade**. The potting mix should be **well drained**. Fertilize monthly with half-strength fertilizer. Pinch the plants back early on to encourage bushy growth.

Tips

Argyranthemums can be used as an accent to specimen plants or to add a colorful splash in mixed containers. They complement many other plants including nemesia, petunia, verbena and bacopa. They are lovely when massed in large container groupings or in window boxes on a sunny ledge.

Recommended

A. fructescens is a compact, rounded plant. It bears single, yellow-centered, daisy-like flowers with white petals. **'Butterfly,'** a Proven Winners Selection, produces canary yellow flowers. **'Gypsy Rose'** bears single, yellow-centered flowers with dark pink petals. The **Molimba Mini Series** has flowers in white, yellow or pink and grows 10–14" tall. **'Summer Melody'** is a top performer with double, dark pink blossoms that fade to lighter pink as they mature. **'Vanilla Butterfly'** bears single, yellow-centered, daisy-like flowers with creamy white petals that are pale yellow at the base.

A. *fructescens* 'Butterfly' with million bells, sedum and others

Cuttings can be taken in late summer and grown indoors over winter to be used the following summer.

Also called: marguerite daisy, cobbity daisy
Features: bushy habit; white, pink or yellow, summer flowers; divided to finely divided foliage **Height:** 10–36" **Spread:** 10–36"
Hardiness: subshrub grown as an annual

Asparagus Fern
Asparagus

A. densiflorus 'Sprengeri' with begonias

Asparagus fern is actually not a fern but a member of the lily family and is closely related to edible asparagus.

Growing
Asparagus fern grows best in **light shade** or **partial shade** but thrives in full sun near the coast. The potting mix should be kept evenly **moist** but allowed to dry out a little between waterings. Fertilize weekly during the growing season with quarter- to half-strength fertilizer. Overwinter indoors or throw away at the end of the season.

Tips
Vigorous growth makes asparagus fern a good filler plant for mixed containers; its unique appearance and habit add an interesting visual element to combinations.

Recommended
A. crispus (basket asparagus) is an airy, graceful plant with bright green, drooping, zigzag stems.

A. densiflorus is an arching, tender perennial with light green, feathery, leaf-like stems. Bright orange to red berries appear in fall. Two cultivars are commonly available. **'Myersii'** (foxtail fern) produces dense, foxtail-like stems 12–18" long. **'Sprengeri'** (emerald fern) has bright green, arching to drooping stems and a loose, open habit. It spreads 3–5' and is often grown where it will have room to hang.

Features: fern-like habit; bright green, needle-like or narrow, leaf-like stems; inconspicuous flowers; inedible, bright orange to red berries
Height: 12–36" **Spread:** 1–5' **Hardiness:** tender perennial grown as an annual

Bacopa
Sutera

S. cordata SNOWSTORM GIANT SNOWFLAKE with African daisy and fan flower

Bacopa grows under and around the stems of taller plants, forming a dense carpet dotted with tiny flowers that eventually drifts over pot edges.

Growing

Bacopa grows best in **partial shade** with protection from the hot afternoon sun. The potting mix should be **moist** and **well drained**. During a drought, bacopa simply drops buds and flowers. Plant with petunias, verbenas or other indicator plants to determine when bacopa needs moisture. Cutting back dead growth may encourage new shoots to form.

Tips

Bacopa is popular for hanging baskets, mixed containers and window boxes. It forms an attractive, spreading mound. Bacopa mixes well with a variety of plants including million bells, geraniums, African daisies and many others.

Recommended

S. cordata forms a dense, compact mound of heart-shaped leaves with scalloped edges and bears tiny, white, star-shaped flowers along neat, trailing stems. **'Cabana Trailing Blue'** bears blue or purple flowers. **'Lavender Showers'** bears pale lavender flowers. **'Olympic Gold'** has gold variegated foliage with white flowers. SNOWSTORM GIANT SNOWFLAKE from Proven Winners is a vigorous plant with large, white flowers. SNOWSTORM PINK has light pink flowers. **'White Surge,'** also from Proven Winners, is a vigorous, late-flowering variety with a mounding habit.

Features: white, lavender, purple, blue or pink flowers; decorative foliage; trailing habit **Height:** 3–6" **Spread:** 12–24" **Hardiness:** tender perennial grown as an annual; can be overwintered near the coast in a protected location

Basil

Ocimum

O. basilicum 'Genovese' and *O. basilicum* 'Cinnamon'

The sweet, fragrant leaves of fresh basil add a delicious, licorice-like flavor to salads and tomato-based dishes.

Growing

Basil grows best in a **warm, sheltered** location in **full sun**. The potting mix should be **moist** and **well drained**. Fertilize weekly with half-strength fertilizer. Pinch tips and remove flower spikes regularly to encourage bushy growth.

Tips

Combine basil in a mixed container with other moisture-loving plants, or consider combining several different types of basil. Place a container of basil next to your potted tomatoes for an Italian-themed garden. Both plants produce the ingredients for bruschetta and other Italian dishes.

Recommended

O. basilicum is one of the most popular culinary herbs. There are dozens of varieties, including ones with large or tiny, green or purple, smooth or ruffled leaves, as well as varied flavors including anise, cinnamon and lemon. **'Green Globe'** forms a rounded mound of tiny leaves. **'Mammoth'** has huge leaves, up to 10" long and about half as wide. **'Purple Ruffles'** has dark purple leaves with frilly margins. **'Siam Queen'** is a cultivar of Thai basil with dark green foliage and dark purple flowers and stems.

Features: bushy habit; fragrant, decorative leaves; pink, purple or white flowers
Height: 12–24" **Spread:** 12–18"
Hardiness: tender annual

Although basil will grow best in a warm spot outdoors, it can also be grown successfully in a bright window indoors to provide you with fresh leaves all year.

Bay Laurel
Laurus

This shrub is an undemanding plant that is happily transferred from a sunny window indoors to a lightly shaded spot outdoors when the weather allows.

Growing

Bay laurel grows well in **light shade, partial shade** or **full sun** in a **sheltered** location. The potting mix should be **moist** and **well drained**. Fertilize monthly during the growing season with half-strength fertilizer. Water when the soil is dry an inch below the surface. A great choice for a Mediterranean garden, bay laurel is not frost tolerant but may overwinter outdoors in a protected spot.

Tips

Bay laurel is an attractive, small shrub that is useful as a structural point in a mixed container and equally attractive when grown as a specimen. It can be pinched back to maintain a compact form or trained as a standard. Combine it with other herbs for a themed container or group of themed containers. Bay laurel tolerates being rootbound and transplants well.

Recommended

L. nobilis is an aromatic, evergreen tree that can grow up to 40' tall where it is hardy. In a container, it stays much smaller and can be pruned to maintain a suitable size. **'Aurea'** has golden yellow foliage.

L. nobilis

Bay leaves are familiar to most of us as the large, flat leaves we pick out of our stews or soups before serving.

Also called: sweet bay **Features:** tender, evergreen shrub; neat habit; undemanding **Height:** 12–36" **Spread:** 8–24" **Hardiness:** zones 8–10

Begonia
Begonia

B. x *tuberhybrida* cultivar with rubber plant, licorice plant, coleus, phormium and lamium

With beautiful flowers, a compact or trailing habit and decorative foliage, there is sure to be a begonia to fulfill your gardening needs. Once for shade gardens only, begonias now include sun varieties as well.

Growing

Most begonias prefer **light to partial shade**, though some can also be planted in full sun. The potting mix should **neutral to acidic, humus rich** and **well drained**. Mix some compost into a peat-based potting mix. Fertilize every two weeks with quarter- to half-strength fertilizer.

The tubers of tuberous begonias can be uprooted when the foliage dies back and stored in slightly moistened peat moss over winter. The tuber will sprout new shoots in late winter and can be potted for another season. Rex begonias can be moved indoors and treated as house-plants in winter.

Tips

All begonias are useful for containers and planters on shaded patios, balconies, decks and porches. The

---

Features: bushy habit; decorative foliage; red, pink, orange, yellow, apricot or white, sometimes bicolored (picotee) flowers
Height: 6–24" **Spread:** 6–24" **Hardiness:** tender perennial grown as an annual

trailing, tuberous varieties can be used in hanging baskets where the flowers can cascade over the edges.

Begonias make great partners for shade-loving fuchsias. They do especially well in moss baskets.

Recommended

B. **Babywing Series** from Proven Winners are sun-tolerant hybrids that include '**Pink**' and '**White**.' They grow 12–15" tall.

B. **Rex Cultorum hybrids** (rex begonias) are dense, mound-forming plants with dramatically patterned, high-contrast variegated foliage in shades of green, red, pink, white, bronze or purple. '**Escargot**' has spiraling, silver-striped, bronzy green leaves. '**Fire Flush**' has red-tinged, green and bronze variegated leaves. '**Fireworks**' has silvery white and purple-banded foliage.

B. x *semperflorens-cultorum* (wax begonias) are compact, mounded plants that have pink, white, red or bicolored flowers and green, bronze, reddish or white variegated foliage. They are more mildew and disease resistant than the tuberous begonias. They bloom continuously with no deadheading needed. '**Buttered Popcorn**,' from Proven Winners, is a heat-tolerant begonia that can be planted in sun or shade. White with a yellow center, it grows 18–36" tall.

B. x *tuberhybrida* (tuberous begonias) form bushy mounds with green, bronze or purple foliage. The flowers can be held upright or in pendulous clusters. Many hybrids are available. **Non-stop Series** begonias are compact, bushy plants with red, yellow, apricot, orange, pink or white, double flowers. Two pendulous selections with flowers in a wide range of colors are '**Chanson**,' with single or semi-double flowers, and '**Illumination**,' with double flowers.

B. hybrid (above), *B.* x *tuberhybrida* cultivar with phormium and others (below)

Bidens

Bidens

B. ferulifolia PETER'S GOLD CARPET

With fern-like foliage and pretty, golden flowers, this plant has a delicate appearance that belies its tough nature.

Growing

Bidens prefers **full sun** but will tolerate partial shade, bearing fewer flowers. The potting mix should be **moist** and **well drained**. Fertilize every two weeks with quarter- to half-strength fertilizer. If plants become lank and unruly in summer, shear them back lightly to encourage new growth and fall flowers.

Tips

Bidens is an absolute must for containers, window boxes and hanging baskets. Its fine foliage and attractive flowers make it useful for filling spaces between other plants.

Recommended

B. ferulifolia is a short-lived perennial that is used as an annual. Tufts of fern-like foliage are tipped with daisy-like, bright yellow flowers. **'Golden Goddess'** bears slightly larger flowers and narrower leaves. PETER'S GOLD CARPET from Proven Winners is a bushy, wide-spreading selection with deep golden yellow flowers. **'Solaire Compact Yellow'** is a low-growing plant with a mounding rather than trailing habit.

Also called: tickseed **Features:** bushy habit; feathery foliage; bright yellow flowers **Height:** 12–24" **Spread:** 12–36" or more **Hardiness:** tender perennial grown as an annual

Black-Eyed Susan

Rudbeckia

R. hirta

Bright and cheerful, black-eyed Susan provides a summer-long display of colorful flowers.

As a cut flower, black-eyed Susan is long lasting in arrangements.

Growing

Black-eyed Susan grows well in **full sun** or **partial shade**. The potting mix should be **well drained**. Water regularly, though plants are fairly drought tolerant. Fertilize monthly with half-strength fertilizer. Pinch plants in June

Features: summer through fall flowers in shades of yellow, orange, brown, red or gold, with brown or green centers **Height:** 1–10' **Spread:** 12–36" **Hardiness:** zones 3–8; biennial or short-lived perennial grown as an annual

R. hirta with dahlia, sedum, fan flower and sedge (above), *R. hirta* 'Irish Eyes' (below)

to encourage shorter, bushier growth. Deadhead to keep the plants neat, to encourage more flower production and to minimize self-seeding.

Tips

Black-eyed Susan is a floriferous addition to mixed containers. It is good to use in containers with wildflower or native themes because it isn't unruly and won't become lank, floppy or messy, as some plants often do if grown in containers. The casual, country look of the blooms makes it a great plant to use in creative or recycled containers such as metal washtubs or old wheelbarrows.

Recommended

R. hirta (gloriosa daisy) forms a bushy mound of bristly foliage and bears bright yellow, daisy-like flowers with brown centers from summer through to the first hard frost in fall. **'Becky'** is a dwarf cultivar that grows up to 12" tall and has large flowers in solid and multi-colored shades of yellow, orange, red or brown. **'Cherokee Sunset'** was a 2002 All-America Selections winner. It bears semi-double and double flowers in all colors. **'Irish Eyes'** bears bright yellow flowers with green centers. This cultivar grows 24–30" tall and is best in large containers where it will not look out of proportion. **Toto Series** are bushy, dwarf cultivars that grow 12–16" tall and bear single flowers with central brown cones and golden orange, lemon yellow or rich mahogany petals.

There are many more hybrids and species. *R. fulgida* var. *sullivantii* **'Goldsturm'** is a low maintenance, long-lived perennial that grows 24–30" tall and bears bright yellow, orange or red, brown-centered flowers. It is powdery mildew resistant. Other species grow 3–6' tall, making them less suitable for containers but worth a try if you want to make a bold statement.

Black-Eyed Susan Vine
Thunbergia

T. alata (far left)

Black-eyed Susan vine is a useful flowering vine whose simple flowers dot the plant, giving it a cheerful, welcoming appearance.

Growing

Black-eyed Susan vine grows well in **full sun, partial shade** or **light shade**. For the most intense flower color, keep plants out of the hot afternoon sun. The potting mix should be **moist** and **well drained** and have some organic matter such as earthworm castings or compost mixed in. Fertilize every two weeks during the growing season with quarter-strength fertilizer.

Tips

Black-eyed Susan vine can be trained to twine around railings and up trellises and small obelisks. It is attractive trailing down from mixed containers and hanging baskets. Pinch the tips to encourage branching. This cottage garden plant mixes beautifully with angelonia and salvia.

Recommended

T. alata is a vigorous, twining climber. It bears yellow flowers, often with dark centers, in summer and fall. **'African Sunset'** has flower colors that range from deep brick red to warm pastel colors to cream. **'Alba'** bears white flowers with dark purple-brown centers. **Suzie Hybrids** bear large flowers in yellow, orange or white. Plant **'Terracotta Skies'** for salmon, mango or terracotta flowers.

Also called: clockvine **Features:** twining, evergreen vine; attractive foliage; yellow, orange, white or sometimes red, summer to fall flowers **Height:** 3–5' **Spread:** 1–5' **Hardiness:** tender perennial grown as an annual

Blood Grass

Imperata

I. cylindrica var. *rubra* with sweet potato vine and spirea

Blood grass appears to glow red when backlit by the sun during the day or by a spotlight at night.

Growing

Blood grass grows best in **full sun** or in **partial shade** in hotter areas. The potting mix should be kept **moist** but not wet. Mix in compost or earthworm castings because this grass likes organic matter in its soil. Fertilize every two weeks during the growing season with quarter-strength fertilizer. Pull out any growth that doesn't turn red because green growth is more vigorous and will tend to dominate. In areas that receive frost, cover containers or move them to a sheltered location in winter.

Tips

Blood grass mixes well in a grass-themed container and makes a good upright companion for bushy and trailing perennials and annuals. Its small size, shallow root system and non-invasive habit are welcome in mixed containers where more vigorous grasses can easily overwhelm other plants. It contrasts well with yellow plants such as marigolds and coreopsis. Add it to pots of bamboo for an Asian-inspired container garden.

Recommended

I. cylindrica var. *rubra* (I. cylindrica 'Red Baron') forms slow-spreading clumps of slender leaves. The grass blades emerge bright green tipped with red that spreads down the leaf as it matures, turning deep wine red by fall, then to copper in winter.

Blood grass is great for brightening up containers, adding color and texture offered by few other plants.

Also called: Japanese blood grass
Features: perennial grass; colorful foliage; slender, upright habit **Height:** 12–18"
Spread: 12" **Hardiness:** zones 4–9

Blue Fescue

Festuca

F. glauca ELIJAH BLUE with Swan River daisy and nemesia

This fine-leaved, ornamental grass forms tufted clumps that resemble pincushions.

Growing

Blue fescue grows well in **full sun** or **partial shade**. The potting mix should be **moist** and **well drained**. Fertilize once a month during the growing season with half-strength fertilizer. This grass is fairly drought tolerant, if you are prone to forgetting to water quite as often as you should. In areas of frost, move fescue containers to a sheltered location out of the wind and sun in winter. Elsewhere, look for the best performance from blue fescue during the cooler months.

Tips

Blue fescue is an interesting accent plant for mixed containers. It adds unusual texture and color to annual and perennial combinations. Try it with plants with contrasting leaves.

Recommended

F. filiformis (fine-leaf fescue) forms a low tuft of bright green, hair-like foliage. It grows 6–8" tall and spreads 8–12".

F. glauca (blue fescue) forms tidy, tufted clumps of fine, blue-toned foliage and produces short spikes of flowers in early summer. Cultivars and hybrids come in varying heights and in shades ranging from blue to olive green. **'Boulder Blue'** and ELIJAH BLUE, a Proven Selection by Proven Winners, have intense blue coloring. **'Skinner's Blue'** is one of the hardiest selections, making it a good choice for container culture.

Features: tuft-forming, perennial grass; silvery or gray-blue to olive green or bright green foliage; spiky or relaxed habit **Height:** 6–12" **Spread:** 8–12" **Hardiness:** zones 3–8

Blue Oat Grass
Helictotrichon

H. sempervirens

$\mathcal{L}$ooking like a giant pincushion, blue oat grass has a strong architectural presence.

Growing
Blue oat grass thrives in **full sun**. The potting mix should be **well drained**. This grass thrives in poor soil and should be fertilized only once at the beginning of summer with half-strength fertilizer. In areas that receive frost, cover containers or move them to a sheltered location in winter. Blue oat grass is evergreen in mild winter areas.

Tips
The bushy, rounded form lends itself perfectly to being grown as a specimen in a large, urn-shaped container. It can also be used as the centerpiece in a mixed container. Blue oat grass is particularly effective with other blue plants such as Russian sage and campanula.

Recommended
H. sempervirens forms a large, dome-shaped clump of narrow, silvery blue leaf blades. Wiry, tan stems emerge from the center of the clump, bearing feathery, tan seedheads. **'Saphirsprudel'** ('Sapphire,' 'Sapphire Fountain') is sometimes described as larger and more intensely blue than the species, but other growers claim they see no difference between the species and the cultivar.

Features: perennial grass; cushion-like habit; brilliant blue foliage; decorative spikes of tan seedheads **Height:** 2–4' **Spread:** 24–30" **Hardiness:** zones 3–9

Bougainvillea

Bougainvillea

Each tiny flower is surrounded by three wavy, papery bracts; the blooms can completely cover the plant.

Growing

Bougainvillea grows best in **full sun** but tolerates partial shade or light shade if it is kept indoors in winter. The potting mix should be **moist** and **well drained**. Mix in compost or earthworm castings. Fertilize every two weeks during the growing season with quarter- to half-strength low-nitrogen fertilizer. In cold areas, this plant can be overwintered indoors or used as an annual. Elsewhere, bougainvillea is a vigorous grower. Go ahead and trim—the bracts form on new wood.

Bougainvillea does not like having its roots disturbed, so take special care when transplanting.

Tips

Bougainvillea is a lovely and adaptable plant as a specimen or when mixed with other plants. It can be trained as a trailing spreader, bushy shrub, standard or climbing vine.

Recommended

***B.* Bambino Series** has compact plants that grow 3–4' tall. It includes **'Baby Alyssa,'** with white bracts and green and white variegated foliage; **'Baby Lauren,'** with lavender bracts and green foliage; **'Baby Sophia,'** with vibrant brick orange bracts; and **'Baby Victoria,'** with magenta bracts and pink, yellow and green variegated foliage. **'Ooh-la-la'** is a tiny spreader, growing only 18" tall but spreading 6–8', with magenta bracts. **'Rosenka'** has unusual gold bracts that turn pink when mature; it grows 3–4' tall and wide.

B. glabra

B. glabra is a tender, evergreen vine with semi-glossy leaves. The bracts are white or magenta and are produced in summer and sometimes again in winter. Where it is hardy, it can grow up to 26' tall. In containers, it can be kept much smaller. **'Raspberry Ice'** has green leaves with irregular, creamy margins. The bracts are bright pink.

Features: evergreen, attractive, sometimes variegated foliage; pink, white, yellow, apricot, red or purple flower bracts **Height:** 8"–8' **Spread:** 1–8' **Hardiness:** zones 9–11; tender vine grown as an annual or overwintered indoors

Bugleweed
Ajuga

A. reptans cultivar with a fern

Bugleweed's shade tolerance makes it particularly welcome in urban settings in places with limited sun exposure, such as on balconies and between buildings.

Growing
Bugleweed develops the best leaf color when grown in **partial shade** or **light shade** but tolerates full shade. Excessive sun may scorch the leaves. The potting mix should be **well drained**. Overwinter outdoors in a sheltered location.

Tips
Bugleweed will spread to fill in the spaces between plants in your mixed containers, and some selections will even trail over the edges of the container. The bold, colorful foliage can be used to create striking contrasts, such as pairing dark-leaved bugleweed with variegated or yellow-leaved hostas.

Recommended
A. pyramidalis 'Metallica Crispa' is slow-growing, with crinkly, bronze foliage and violet-blue flowers.

A. reptans is a low, quick-spreading plant with many colorful cultivars, such as 'Burgundy Glow,' 'Caitlin's Giant' and 'Multicolor.'

A. x tenorii is a hybrid with small leaves, a somewhat trailing habit and deep blue flowers. The cultivars 'Chocolate Chip,' 'Toffee Chip' and 'Vanilla Chip' are available.

Features: evergreen perennial; purple, pink, bronze, green, white, often variegated foliage; late-spring to early-summer flowers in purple, blue, pink or white **Height:** 3–12" **Spread:** 6–36" **Hardiness:** zones 3–8

Calla Lily
Zantedeschia

Z. elliottiana hybrid with pansies

Calla lilies are exotic and elegant and lend a tropical touch to your container garden. Solid and bicolor shades of pink, purple, orange-red and yellow have joined the traditional white.

Growing

Where summers are cool, grow calla lilies in **full sun** in a **sheltered** location. In warmer areas, they like bright light with afternoon shade. The potting mix should be **moist** and **well drained** until the leaves have begun to unfurl. Once plants are actively growing, the soil can be kept quite wet. Fertilize every two weeks with quarter- to half-strength fertilizer. Deadhead the faded flowers and stems.

In zones 8 and above, slowly reduce the water toward the end of summer to encourage dormancy and allow the foliage to die back. After a light frost, remove the foliage and stems from the

Features: clump-forming habit; glossy, green foliage; summer flowers **Height:** 16–36" **Spread:** 8–24" **Hardiness:** tender, rhizomatous perennial grown as an annual

rhizome, being careful not to damage it. Wash the rhizome gently under tepid water, removing soil and debris. Dust the rhizome with a fungicide and leave it to dry for a week at room temperature in a well-ventilated room. Once cured, store the rhizome in a paper bag in a cool, dark location at 41–50° F until it's time to plant it again in spring. You can also mulch the container with bark or straw and move it to a sheltered area.

Tips

Calla lilies are stunning additions to large, colorful, mixed or specimen containers. For a theme garden, combine them with other water-loving plants such as elephant ears, rush and sweet flag to create a potted bog garden.

Recommended

Z. aethiopica forms a clump of glossy, green, arrow-shaped leaves. Ornamental white spathes surround the creamy yellow flower spikes. Cultivars and hybrids are available.

Z. elliottiana (yellow calla, golden calla) forms a clump of white-spotted, dark green, heart-shaped leaves. Yellow spathes surround bright yellow flower spikes. This species is the parent plant of many popular hybrids.

Z. rehmannii (pink arum, pink calla) forms a clump of narrow, dark green leaves. White, pink or purple spathes surround yellow flower spikes. This species is also the parent of many hybrids. Look for dwarf varieties growing 12–18" tall; some have speckled foliage.

Z. elliottiana hybrid with petunia, canna lily, dracaena and Swan River daisy (above)
Z. elliottiana hybrid (below)

Don't store all the rhizomes you lift in fall; these plants grow vigorously, and you may need only a few pieces for the following summer. The rest can be given to friends and family or composted.

Canna Lily
Canna

Canna lilies are stunning, dramatic plants that give an exotic flair to any garden.

Growing

Canna lilies grow best in **full sun**. The potting mix should be **moist** and **well drained**. Fertilize every two weeks with quarter- to half-strength fertilizer. Deadhead regularly to prolong blooming. Once all of the buds have opened and the flowers are finished, remove the stalk down to the next side shoot.

In frost-prone areas, dig up the rhizomes and air-dry them. Lay them flat and just barely cover them with soil or store them in paper bags in a cool, dry spot. Transplant canna lilies earlier than June to ensure they will flower before the end of the season.

Tips

Canna lilies can be included in large planters. They can be grown in containers of mixed canna lily varieties or used as focal points with bushy and trailing annuals.

Recommended

A wide range of canna lilies are available, including cultivars and hybrids with green, bronze, purple or yellow-and-green-striped foliage. Flowers may be white, red, orange, pink, yellow or sometimes bicolored. **Pfitzer Series** has dwarf selections that grow about 36" tall.

C. hybrid with lobelia

The silvery foliage of dusty miller and licorice plant creates an excellent backdrop for the colorful canna lily. Pairing coleus with canna lily gives a container a bold, tropical look.

Features: green, blue-green, bronze, purple, yellow, sometimes variegated foliage; red, white, orange, pink, yellow or sometimes bicolored flowers **Height:** 3–7' **Spread:** 18–36" **Hardiness:** zones 7–11; tender, rhizomatous perennial grown as an annual

Catch-Fly
Silene

S. pendula 'Peach Blossom'

Catch-fly helps keep pest populations down by attracting beneficial insects and even by catching small insects on its sticky stems and leaves, which makes it a favorite with children.

The flowers of this plant are attractive to hummingbirds, butterflies and other pollinating insects.

Growing
Catch-fly grows well in **full sun** or **light shade**. The potting mix should be **moist** and **well drained**. Fertilize every two weeks with quarter- to half-strength fertilizer.

Tips
Catch-fly makes a good filler plant in mixed containers. This annual may turn up in your containers year after year because it tends to self-seed.

Recommended
S. armeria (sweet William catch-fly) forms a basal rosette of gray-green leaves from which many sticky stems emerge. It bears clusters of vivid pink flowers. **'Electra'** bears more flower clusters than the species.

S. coeli-rosa (rose-of-heaven) is an upright plant with slender, gray-green foliage. Flowers are bright pink with paler, often white centers. **'Blue Angel'** bears blue flowers. **'Rose Angel'** bears bright pink flowers.

S. pendula (nodding catch-fly) is a low-growing, bushy, mounding or spreading plant. It bears loose clusters of nodding, single or double, light pink flowers. **'Peach Blossom'** has flowers that open a deep pink and gradually fade to white as they mature, with flowers in different stages of coloration showing at once. **'Snowball'** bears double, white flowers.

Features: bushy, spreading or upright habit; loose or dense clusters of deep to light pink or white flowers **Height:** 6–24"
Spread: 6–18" **Hardiness:** annual

Cilantro • Coriander

Coriandrum

The delicate, cloud-like clusters of flowers attract pollinating insects such as butterflies and bees as well as abundant predatory insects that will help keep pest insects at a minimum in your garden.

Growing

This herb prefers **full sun** but tolerates partial shade. The potting mix should be **light** and **well drained**. Fertilize monthly with half-strength fertilizer. This plant dislikes humid conditions and does best during a dry summer. In warm areas, it does best during late winter and early spring.

Tips

This species has pungent leaves and is best planted where people will not have to brush past it. It is, however, a delight to behold when in flower and is an excellent plant for adding volume to your mixed planters. The airy clouds of white flowers create a lovely backdrop for bright red, pink or purple flowers.

Recommended

C. sativum forms a clump of lacy basal foliage above which large, loose clusters of tiny, white flowers are produced. The seeds ripen in late summer and fall.

C. sativum is a popular culinary herb. The leaves, called cilantro, are used in salads, salsas and soups, and the seeds, called coriander, are used in pies, chutneys and marmalades. The flavor of each is quite distinct.

C. sativum

Features: form; foliage; flowers; seeds
Height: 16–24" **Spread:** 8–16"
Hardiness: tender annual

Citrus

Citrus

C. x *meyeri* 'Dwarf Meyer'

Growing a citrus tree in a container has many advantages. You can control the soil, drainage and temperature requirements and position it where you can enjoy the fragrant blossoms as well as the fruit.

Growing

Citrus trees like **full sun**. The potting mix should be **light** and **well drained**. When planting, position the root collar above and the root crown barely below the soil line. Water infrequently but

deeply and do not overwater. Fertilize with a high-nitrogen fertilizer. In cold winter areas, bring the container inside and position it near a bright window.

Replant your tree as it gets larger. Starting out with a container that is too large interferes with moisture requirements.

Tips

Citrus trees make a strong vertical statement in Mediterranean-themed gardens. Lemons, oranges, limes and grapefruits are all available in dwarf varieties that are perfect for containers.

Because it's easy to over- or underwater a citrus, consider investing in a moisture meter. This device can also reduce bloom drop, which is often caused by inconsistent watering.

Recommended

C. aurantifolia **'Bearss Seedless Lime'** does well in cool areas and bears fruit all year.

C. limon **'Eureka'** is a traditional lemon available as a dwarf that produces tasty, tart fruit year-round.

C. x *meyeri* **'Improved Meyer'** is a hardy cross between a lemon and mandarin orange. Its sweet, juicy, thin-skinned fruit makes it a cook's favorite. It does not need as much heat as other varieties to bloom. Naturally small, it is an ideal container choice.

C. paradisi **'Cocktail Grapefruit,'** a cross between a mandarin orange and a pomelo, produces sweet, low-acid fruit. **'Oroblanco Grapefruit'** requires less heat than other varieties and produces sweet, seedless fruit in the middle of winter.

Features: fruiting tree; fragrant blossoms
Height: 6–10' in containers **Spread:** 4–8' in containers **Hardiness:** zones 9–10

Clematis
Clematis

C. alpina

Climbing vines can be truly stunning growing up an obelisk or other trellis from a container. New clematis varieties bred specifically for containers make this easier than ever.

Growing

Clematis prefers **full sun** but tolerates full shade. Try to keep the container in the shade because this plant does best when its roots stay cool. The potting mix should be **moist** and **well drained** and have some organic matter such as compost mixed in. Fertilize every two weeks during the growing season with quarter- to half-strength fertilizer.

This hardy plant has sensitive roots. Freezing and thawing will more likely kill your clematis vine than extreme

---

Features: twining vine or bushy perennial; attractive, leafy habit; flowers in shades of blue, purple, pink, white, yellow or red or sometimes bicolored **Height:** 1–5' **Spread:** 1–4' **Hardiness:** zones 3–8

C. x jackmanii (above), C. integrifolia (below)

cold. Where winters are cold, move the container to a location where the temperature will stay fairly even.

Tips

Clematis makes a lovely addition to a mixed container, where you can grow it up an obelisk or trellis or let it spill over the edge. The abundant flowers make this plant worth including in your containers even if it survives only a few years. To keep the roots cool, add mulch, plant a low-growing groundcover or intermix with a taller plant that shades the roots. Clematis and roses are a beautiful tried-and-true combination.

Recommended

C. alpina (alpine clematis) is a twining vine that blooms in spring and early summer, bearing bell-shaped, blue flowers with white centers.

C. integrifolia (solitary clematis) is a bushy perennial rather than a climbing vine, though it has flexible, trailing growth that can be trained to grow up a low trellis or spill over the edge of a container. It bears flared, bell-shaped, purple flowers in summer.

C. x jackmanii (Jackman clematis) is a twining vine that bears large, purple flowers in summer. Many hybrids are available, with flowers in a wide range of colors.

C. viticella **Raymond Evison Patio Clematis™ Collection** are slow-growing, twining, compact vines that grow 3–4' tall and 18–36" wide and are hardy to zone 4. The cultivars **'Angelique,' 'Parisienne,' 'Chantilly,' 'Cezanne,' 'Picardy,' 'Versailles'** and **'Bourbon'** bloom well into fall in varied shades of magenta, purple and purple-blue.

Combine two clematis selections together to provide a mix of tone and texture.

Cleome

Cleome

Create a bold, exotic display in your garden with these lovely and unusual flowers.

Growing

Cleome prefers **full sun** but tolerates partial shade. The potting mix should be **moist** and **well drained**. These plants are drought tolerant but look and perform best if watered regularly. Fertilize monthly with quarter-strength fertilizer. Pinch out the center of the plant when transplanting, and it will branch out to produce up to a dozen blooms. Deadhead to prolong the blooming period. Cleome is especially hardy in warm inland areas.

Tips

Cleome is an interesting plant to use as the central or focal plant in a mixed container.

Recommended

C. hassleriana is a tall, upright plant with strong, supple, thorny stems. The foliage and flowers have a strong, but pleasant, scent. Flowers are borne in loose, rounded clusters at the ends of leafy stems. **'Helen Campbell'** has white flowers. **Royal Queen Series** bear fade-resistant flowers in all colors. **'Sparkler Blush'** is a dwarf cultivar that grows up to 36" tall. It bears pink flowers that fade to white. The hybrid **Spirit Series** from Proven Winners, for zones 8–10, has durable container plants that grow 24–30" tall and is available in **'Appleblossom,'** with light pink blooms; **'Frost,'** with snow-white blossoms; violet-hued **'Violeta'**; **'Damask,'** featuring rose-pink flowers; and **'Merlot,'** whose burgundy blossoms provide attractive contrast to others in the series.

C. hassleriana with nicotiana, geranium and impatiens

C. serrulata (Rocky Mountain bee plant) is native to western North America. It is rarely available commercially. The thornless dwarf cultivar **'Solo'** is available to be grown from seed. It grows 12–18" tall and bears pink and white blooms.

Also called: spider flower **Features:** bushy, upright habit; scented, divided foliage; pink, rose, violet or white flower clusters **Height:** 1–5' **Spread:** 18–36" **Hardiness:** annual

Clover

Trifolium

T. repens 'Dark Dancer' with coleus and others

Growing

Clover is best grown in **full sun** or **partial shade**. The potting mix should be **moist, well drained** and **neutral**. Fertilize once during the growing season, about a month after you plant it out, with half-strength fertilizer. In areas that receive frost, move it to a sheltered location in winter or throw it away after the first frost and plant new clover the following summer.

Tips

This lovely little plant will add interest to mixed containers. It is especially striking when grouped with other plants with dramatically colored foliage or bright, contrasting flowers.

Recommended

T. repens is a low, spreading perennial often grown as an annual. It is rarely grown in favor of the many attractive cultivars. The small, rounded flower clusters can be pink, red, yellow or white. **'Dark Dancer'** ('Atropurpureum') has a dwarf habit and dark burgundy leaves with lime green margins. **'Salsa Dancer'** produces bright green foliage with burgundy and white markings in the center of each leaf and bears white flowers.

Because of its small stature, clover can be lost to the eye when mixed with other plants in beds but seems to stand out when planted in containers, both as a specimen and when mixed with other annuals.

Because of its invasive nature, clover is ideally suited to container culture. You can control the roots of clover and other ornamental groundcovers in containers by inserting chipped saucers or small plates into the soil to serve as an underground root barrier. Let the top half of the crockery poke above the soil as a charming accent in the pot.

Features: spreading habit; decorative, often variegated foliage; small, globe-shaped, white, pink, red or yellow flowers **Height:** 3–12" **Spread:** 12–18" or more **Hardiness:** zones 4–8; perennial grown as an annual

Coleus

Solenostemon (Coleus)

Coleus has always been available in a great range of colors, and it is only more desirable as new varieties emerge onto the market in colors such as plum, burgundy, chartreuse, gold, lime, copper, wine and almost black. Exciting new coleus for sun extends this dramatic, colorful plant beyond the shade garden.

Growing

Coleus grows best in **partial shade** or **full sun** depending on the variety. The potting mix should be **humus rich, moist** and **well drained**. Mix in some compost or earthworm castings. When flower buds develop, it is best to pinch them off because the plants tend to stretch out and become less attractive after they flower.

These plants are perennials that are grown as annuals, but they also make attractive houseplants. Cuttings taken from favorites in late summer can be grown indoors in a bright room by a sunny window.

Tips

The bold, colorful foliage creates a dramatic display when several different selections are grouped together in a single container or group of containers. Coleus also makes an excellent accent plant in a mixed container with other annuals or perennials.

Recommended

S. scutellarioides (*Coleus blumei* var. *verschaffeltii*) cultivars and hybrids form

S. scutellarioides SEDONA

Coleus can be trained into a tree form. Pinch off the lower leaves and side branches as they grow to create a long, bare stem with leaves on only the upper half. Once the plant reaches the desired height, pinch from the top to create a bushy, rounded crown.

Features: bushy habit; colorful, often variegated foliage in shades of green, yellow, pink, red, burgundy or purple **Height:** 6–36" **Spread:** 6–24" **Hardiness:** tender perennial grown as an annual

bushy mounds of foliage. The leaf edges range from slightly toothed to very ruffled. The leaves are usually multi-colored with shades ranging from pale greenish yellow to deep purple-black. Plants grow 6–36" tall, depending on the cultivar, and the spread is usually equal to the height. Some interesting cultivars include **'Black Prince,'** with deep purple, almost black foliage; **'Fishnet Stockings,'** with purple-veined, bright green foliage; **'Merlin's Magic,'** with deeply divided, slightly ruffled, purple, pink, burgundy or yellow and green variegated foliage; and SEDONA, a Proven Selection by Proven Winners, with pink-veined, orange foliage. The **Colorblaze Series** from Proven Winners maintain color in full sun to full shade. Look for **'Dark Star,'** with compact, dark purple foliage; **'Dipt in Wine,'** which has burgundy leaves with a gold base; and the compact **'LifeLime,'** with chartreuse foliage.

S. scutellarioides cultivar with begonia and fig (above)
S. scutellarioides cultivar with coral bells and others (below)

Coral Bells
Heuchera

From soft yellow-greens and oranges to midnight purples and silvery, dappled maroons, coral bells offer a great variety of foliage options.

Growing

Coral bells grow best in **light shade** or **partial shade**. Foliage colors can bleach out in full sun. The potting mix should be **neutral to alkaline, moist** and **well drained**. Mix in some compost or earthworm castings. Fertilize once a month during the growing season with quarter- to half-strength fertilizer. Cover or move to a sheltered location in winter.

H. AMBER WAVES, from Proven Winners, alone and with African daisy, in front of sedge (above), *H.* hybrid with sweet potato vine, begonia and sweet flag (below)

Also called: heuchera, alum root
Features: mound-forming or spreading perennial; scalloped or heart-shaped, colorful foliage; red, pink, purple, white or yellow, small, summer flowers **Height:** 1–4'
Spread: 12–18" **Hardiness:** zones 3–8

Tips

Coral bells make attractive additions to mixed containers. The colorful foliage contrasts particularly well with grasses, ferns and yellow-flowered plants such as lady's mantle, iris and dahlia. Combine different selections of coral bells for an interesting display. The persistent foliage of coral bells is excellent for providing much-needed color for winter container gardens. Colors deepen in cold weather.

Recommended

There are many hybrids and cultivars of coral bells available. The following are just a few of the possibilities. **'Caramel'** has apricot-colored foliage and pink flowers. **'Chocolate Ruffles'** has ruffled, glossy brown foliage with purple undersides that give the leaves a bronzed appearance. **'Coral Cloud'** forms a clump of glossy, crinkled leaves and bears pinkish red flowers. **'Firefly'** develops a clump of dark green leaves with attractive, fragrant, bright pinkish red flowers. Both **'Lime Rickey'** and DOLCE KEY LIME PIE from Proven Winners form a low mass of chartreuse leaves. **'Marmalade'** has foliage that emerges red and matures to orange-yellow. **'Montrose Ruby'** has bronzy purple foliage with bright red undersides. **'Northern Fire'** has red flowers and leaves mottled with silver. **'Obsidian'** has lustrous, dark purple, nearly black foliage. **'Pewter Veil'** has silvery purple leaves with dark gray veins. Its flowers are white flushed with pink. **'Velvet Night'** has dark purple leaves with a metallic sheen and creamy white flowers.

Coral bells are delicate-looking woodland plants and can be combined with other woodland plants such as ferns to create a themed container.

H. DOLCE KEY LIME PIE with sedge and African daisy

Crocosmia

Crocosmia

The intense colors of crocosmia are a beacon in the garden and create a brilliant display in a container.

Growing

Crocosmias prefer **full sun** in a **sheltered** location. The potting mix should be **humus rich, moist** and **well drained**. Fertilize monthly during the growing season with half-strength fertilizer. Move plants to a sheltered location and mulch in winter. These plants will be short-lived in containers.

Tips

These attractive, unusual plants create a striking display when planted by themselves in large containers or in mixed containers with other perennials.

Recommended

C. x *crocosmiflora* is a spreading plant with long, strap-like leaves. It grows 18–36" tall, and the clump spreads about 12". One-sided spikes of red, orange or yellow flowers are borne in mid- and late summer. **'Citronella'** ('Golden Fleece') bears bright yellow flowers.

C. **'Little Redhead'** features tomato red blooms with yellow throats and grows 18–24" tall.

C. **'Lucifer'** is the hardiest of the bunch and bears bright scarlet flowers. It grows 3–4' tall, with a spread of about 18".

If you've had no luck overwintering crocosmia, the problem may be that the corms get too wet. Drag the pot to a dry spot such as under the eaves or beneath a patio table for winter. Also, the corms can be dug up in fall and stored in slightly damp peat moss in a cool, dark place during winter.

C. 'Lucifer'

Features: cormous, semi-tender perennial; bright green, strap-like leaves; red, orange or yellow flowers in mid- to late summer
Height: 18"–4' **Spread:** 12–18"
Hardiness: zones 5–9

Cuphea
Cuphea

C. FLAMENCO RUMBA

This wonderful plant will attract hummingbirds and butterflies to your garden.

Growing
When planted in a container, cuphea grows well in **partial shade**. The potting mix should be **moist** and **well drained**. Short periods of drought are tolerated.

Features: tropical shrub; red, pink, purple, violet, green or white flowers **Height:** 6–24" **Spread:** 10–36" **Hardiness:** tender shrub grown as an annual

Fertilize monthly during the growing season with half-strength fertilizer. This plant is frost tender and can be grown as an annual or brought indoors at the end of summer and treated like a houseplant.

Tips
This is a good plant for container gardens with a tropical theme because it grows well with canna lily, banana and other plants with hot, bright colors.

Recommended
C. hyssopifolia (Mexican heather, false heather, elfin herb) is a bushy, branching plant that forms a flat-topped mound. The flowers have green calyces and light purple, pink or sometimes white petals. The plants bloom from summer to frost. **'Allyson Purple'** ('Allyson') is a dwarf plant that bears lavender flowers. **'Desert Snow'** has white flowers.

C. ignea (*C. platycentra*; cigar flower, firecracker plant) is a spreading, freely branching plant that weaves attractively through mixed plantings. Thin, tubular, bright red flowers are produced from late spring to frost. Cultivars include **'David Verity,'** with large, reddish orange blossoms on spikes that grow 24" tall, and **'Petite Peach,'** with delicate peach blooms. It can also be used as a houseplant.

C. llavea (bat face, bunny ears, tiny mice) hybrids include the FLAMENCO SERIES, Proven Selections from Proven Winners. FLAMENCO TANGO has bright purple-pink flowers. FLAMENCO RUMBA bears fiery red flowers with dark purple centers. New compact, early-blooming **'Totally Tempted'** grows 10–12" tall in zones 9–11 and bears lively red flowers with lavender throats.

Dahlia
Dahlia

D. hybrid with zinnia, nasturtium and thyme

The variation in size, shape and color of dahlia flowers is astonishing. Special varieties bred for containers fit neatly into all types of potted landscapes.

Growing

Dahlias like **full sun** with afternoon shade in hot areas. The potting mix should be **humus rich, moist** and **well drained**. Fertilize every two weeks during the growing season with quarter-strength, low-nitrogen fertilizer. Deadhead to keep plants neat and to encourage more blooms. Be vigilant about snails, slugs and spider mites.

The tubers can be lifted in fall and stored over winter in slightly moist peat moss. Pot them and keep them in a bright room when they start sprouting in mid- to late winter. Bring them outside after the danger of frost has passed. Along the coast and in areas that don't

Features: bushy habit; attractive foliage; summer flowers in shades of red, yellow, orange, pink, purple, white or sometimes bicolored **Height:** 8"–5' **Spread:** 8–24" **Hardiness:** tender, tuberous perennial usually grown as an annual

D. 'Chic' (above), *D.* hybrids with lobelia and dracaena (below)

drop much below 40° F, you can over-winter dahlias outdoors in a dry spot.

Tips

The sturdy, bushy growth of dahlias gives them a shrubby appearance that can be used to visually anchor a mixed container that includes softer-looking or trailing plants. The stunning flowers draw the eye and create a strong focal point, so use them in places you want people to see or notice. When using the taller dahlias in a large pot, you can support the heavy blooms with a wire tomato cage, or surround the plants with the some stiff upright plants such as *Sedum* 'Autumn Joy.'

Recommended

D. hybrids are bushy, tuberous peren-nials with glossy leaves in shades of green, bronze or purple. They are gener-ally described by their flower shape, such as collarette, decorative or peony-flowered. The flowers are 2–12" across and are available in shades of purple, pink, white, yellow, orange, red or bicol-ored. Look for varieties that stand 12–20" high and require little if any support. **'Amazon Pink and Rose'** is a miniature plant with yellow-centered, pink, semi-double flowers. The petals are light pink with deep pink bases. **'Bishop of Llandaff'** has dark red, semi-double flowers and bronze foliage. **'Dalstar Yellow'** is a miniature plant with pale yellow, semi-double flowers. **'Dalina Mini Bahamas'** is a dwarf plant with glossy, green foliage and fuchsia pink, double flowers. **'David Howard'** has multi-tonal orange, double flowers that contrast with its dark purple foliage. **'Melody Allegro,'** the American Dahlia Society Container/Border of the Year for 2006, is an unusual combina-tion of orange, pink, salmon and lilac that grows to 24" tall with 4½" wide blooms.

Daylily
Hemerocallis

The daylily's adaptability and durability, combined with its variety in color, blooming period, size and texture, explain its popularity.

Growing

Daylilies grow in any light from **full sun to full shade**. The deeper the shade, the fewer flowers will be produced. The potting mix should be **moist** and **well drained**, but these plants tolerate both wet and dry conditions. Fertilize monthly during the growing season with half-strength fertilizer. Deadhead to encourage more flowering. Move containers to a sheltered location in winter.

Tips

Plant daylilies alone, or group them in containers. Although the small selections seem best suited to container culture, the larger plants make a bold statement and will grow equally well in containers.

Recommended

Daylilies come in an almost infinite number of sizes and colors over the range of species, cultivars and hybrids. They all form clumps of strap-like foliage and produce a cluster of buds on a stem that is held above the foliage. The buds open one at a time, and each lasts for a single day. **'Seagold'** is a dwarf with amber-peach flowers that grows to 22" tall and blooms repeatedly throughout the summer. **'Stella D'oro'** is a dwarf ever-blooming daylily perfect for pots.

H. 'Stella D'oro'

More than 12,000 daylily selections have been developed, with sometimes hundreds more added yearly.

Features: clump-forming perennial; grass-like foliage; spring and summer flowers in every color except blue and pure white **Height:** 1–4' **Spread:** 1–4' **Hardiness:** zones 2–11

Diascia
Diascia

D. 'Trailing Antique Rose'

Growing

Diascia grows well in **full sun** or **partial shade** and blooms most prolifically during cooler weather. The potting mix should be **moist** and **well drained**. Fertilize weekly with quarter- to half-strength fertilizer. Although disacia does not require deadheading, shearing spent stems will promote another flush of bloom. Some varieties are frost tolerant, giving them a year-round bloom cycle.

Tips

Available in trailing and upright versions, diascia mixes well with bacopa, million bells, coral bells, nemesia and many others.

Recommended

D. **Flying Colors Series** from Proven Winners have intense colors and large flowers. **'Appleblossom'** has white and pink bicolored flowers in early spring. **'Apricot'** has dark green foliage and flowers the color of ripe apricot. **'Coral,'** with its bright coral flowers, is the most heat-tolerant in the series. Vibrant **'Orange'** thrives in both heat and humidity. **'Red'** has large blooms with dark red throats in a more upright habit. **'Trailing Antique Rose'** has deep rose flowers and a semi-trailing habit.

A member of the snapdragon family, diascia has delicate, loose spikes in colors that look fantastic in mixed combinations as well as in single-plant hanging baskets.

This plant draws its common name, twinspur, from the two distinctive "spurs" at the top of each flower.

Also called: twinspur **Features:** snapdragon-like flowers in loose spikes in solid and bicolor shades of pink, red and orange **Height:** 8–12" **Spread:** 8–10" **Hardiness:** annual grown as perennial in zones 7–10

Dogwood

Cornus

C. sericea 'Isanti'

Flowers, stem color, leaf variegation, fall color, growth habit, adaptability and hardiness are all positive attributes to be found in dogwoods. This lovely small tree does best in cooler areas to zone 8.

Growing

Dogwoods grow well in **full sun, light shade** or **partial shade**, with a slight preference for light shade. The potting

Move dogwoods to an unheated garage or shed in winter, especially in areas where the ground freezes.

Features: deciduous large shrub or small tree; attractive, late-spring to early-summer flowers; fall foliage; stem color; fruit **Height:** 3–10' in containers **Spread:** 2–8' in containers **Hardiness:** zones 2–8

C. alba 'Bud's Yellow' (above), *C. alba* 'Bailhalo' (below)

mix should be **humus rich, neutral to slightly acidic** and **well drained**. Mix in compost or earthworm castings and fertilize monthly during the growing season with quarter-strength fertilizer. Move containers to a sheltered location in winter.

Tips

If you have very large containers or planters and want to grow a shrub or small tree, dogwoods are a good choice, though they may need a bit more pruning and training than they would in a garden. The larger dogwoods will probably outgrow a container and need to be moved to a garden in about three to five years, unless you root prune them every two or so years.

Recommended

C. alba (red-twig dogwood, Tartarian dogwood) and *C. sericea* (*C. stolonifera*; red-osier dogwood) species and cultivars are grown for their bright red stems that provide winter interest. Cultivars are available with stems in varied shades of red, orange or yellow. Fall foliage color can also be attractive.

C. alternifolia (pagoda dogwood) can be grown as a large, multi-stemmed shrub or a small, single-stemmed tree. The branches have an attractive, layered appearance. Clusters of small, white flowers appear in early summer. The cultivar **'Argentia'** has silver and green variegated leaves. (Zones 3–8)

C. kousa (Kousa dogwood) is grown for its decorative flowers, fruit, fall color and interesting bark. The white-bracted flowers are followed by bright red fruit. The foliage turns red and purple in fall. **'Satomi'** has soft pink flowers. (Zones 5–8)

Dusty Miller

Senecio

S. cineraria 'Silver Dust'

usty miller makes an artful addition to container gardens. The soft, silvery gray, deeply lobed foliage creates a good backdrop to show off the brightly colored flowers or foliage of other plants.

Growing

Dusty miller prefers **full sun** but tolerates light shade. The potting mix should be **well drained**. Fertilize no more than once a month during the growing season with quarter-strength fertilizer. Pinch off the flowers before they bloom; the flowers aren't showy and steal energy that would otherwise go to the foliage.

Dusty miller will overwinter in mild winter areas near the coast. Don't prune it until March, and then cut back the winter-weary foliage almost to the ground. By June, the plants will look fresh with new growth.

Tips

The soft, silvery, lacy leaves of dusty miller are its main feature, and it is used primarily as a contrast or backdrop plant.

Recommended

S. cineraria forms a mound of fuzzy, silvery gray, lobed or finely divided foliage. Many cultivars have been developed. **'Cirrus'** has lobed, silvery green or white foliage. **'Silver Dust'** has deeply lobed, silvery white foliage. **'Silver Lace'** has delicate, silvery white foliage that glows in the moonlight.

Features: bushy habit; variably lobed foliage in shades of silvery gray **Height:** 12–24"
Spread: equal to height or slightly narrower
Hardiness: tender annual

Dwarf Morning Glory
Convolvulus

C. tricolor

If you love morning glory but don't want a climber, try this little cutie in containers and window boxes.

Growing

Dwarf morning glory prefers **full sun**. The potting mix must be **well drained**. Fertilize no more than once, about a month after planting, with quarter-strength fertilizer. This plant will produce lots of foliage but few flowers in soil that is too fertile.

Tips

Dwarf morning glory is a compact, mounding plant that can be grown in containers and hanging baskets. It makes a nice plant to grow alone in a small container and also mixes well with other annuals. The mounding to slightly trailing form looks good when combined with grasses.

Recommended

C. tricolor is a compact, mound-forming plant that bears trumpet-shaped flowers that last only a single day, opening in the morning and twisting shut that evening. **Ensign Series** has low-growing, spreading plants that grow about 6" tall. **'Royal Ensign'** has deep blue flowers with white and yellow throats. **'Star of Yalta'** bears deep purple flowers that pale to violet in the throat.

Although this plant is related to the noxious weed C. arvensis *(bindweed), dwarf morning glory is not invasive or problematic.*

Features: mound-forming habit; blue, purple or pink, summer flowers sometimes variegated with yellow and white throats **Height:** 6–16" **Spread:** 10–12" **Hardiness:** annual

Echeveria

Echeveria

*P*opular for succulent container gardens, rosette-forming echeveria comes in a wide variety of leaf colors and shapes. Although grown primarily for its foliage, echeveria does flower in summer, usually in shades of pink, red or coral.

Growing

Echeveria grows well in **full sun** or **partial shade**. The potting mix should be **well drained**. Water only when dry. Although it tolerates drought and likes heat, it may need some water during the summer, and some varieties may burn in hot summer areas. In areas that dip to 25° F, move potted echeveria to a sheltered location in winter.

Tips

These low-maintenance plants look great in shallow bowls combined with other water-conserving plants such as aloe and agave.

Recommended

E. **hybrids** from Proven Winners' new **Retro Succulents** line include many unusual selections. Look for **'Afterglow,'** a sun-lover with powdery lavender leaves, and **'Red Glo,'** whose gray-green leaves have a pinkish cast with bright red leaf margins. Flowers are lime green with light pink margins.

E. racemosa **'Brown Sugar'** has long, narrow, two-toned leaves—mahogany on top, pink on bottom.

E. runyonii **'Topsy Turvy'** has unusual, pale blue, spoon-shaped, twisty leaves and yellow or orange, tubular flowers that attract hummingbirds. It grows 6–8" tall and spreads 8–12".

E. 'Afterglow' with others

E. subrigida **'Fire and Ice'** from Proven Winners was named to *Garden Design*'s Way Hot 100 list for 2008 and sports sea-foam leaves with red margins.

Features: clumping, rosette-forming succulent with attractive, summer flowers **Height:** 3–16" **Spread:** 8–12" **Hardiness:** zones 9–11; usually grown as an annual

Elder

Sambucus

S. *nigra* BLACK BEAUTY with African daisy, coral bells and euphorbia (above), S. *nigra* BLACK LACE (below)

Features: large, bushy, deciduous shrub; early-summer flowers; edible fruit; colorful, decorative foliage **Height:** 2–10' in containers **Spread:** 2–10' in containers **Hardiness:** zones 3–8

Elder is a versatile shrub that can be trained to function as a small tree in a container garden.

Growing

Elders grow well in **full sun** or **partial shade**. Yellow-leaved cultivars and varieties develop the best color in light shade or partial shade, and black-, burgundy- or purple-leaved cultivars develop the best color in full sun. The potting mix should be **moist** and **well drained**. Fertilize monthly during summer with quarter-strength fertilizer. Stop fertilizing by fall to give the plant time to harden off for winter.

Move containers to a sheltered location for winter or cover the plants to protect them from wind and temperature fluctuations. Prune elders back in spring to keep them at a suitable size. New growth emerges from stumps. You may have to root prune them every few years or move them to a garden when they become too large for the container.

Tips

Elders make a strong architectural statement and are best suited to large containers. Train them as small, single- or multi-stemmed trees. Plant annuals with contrasting flower colors around the base of an elder for an eye-catching combination.

Recommended

S. canadensis (American elder), **S. nigra** (black elder) and **S. racemosa** (European red elder) are rounded shrubs with white or pink flowers followed by red or dark purple berries. Cultivars are available with green, yellow, bronze or purple, deeply divided or feathery foliage. *S. canadensis* **'Lanciniata'** has lacy, green foliage that gives this shrub a fern-like or feathery appearance. *S. nigra* BLACK BEAUTY, a Proven Winners Color Choice Selection, has dark purple, almost black, foliage that darkens as summer progresses. *S. nigra* BLACK LACE, another Proven Winners Color Choice Selection, produces finely cut black foliage and pink flowers. *S. nigra* **'Madonna'** bears dark green foliage with wide, irregular, yellow margins. *S. racemosa* **'Sutherland Gold'** has deeply divided, yellow-green foliage.

Elderberries will attract birds to your garden.

S. *nigra* 'Madonna' (above)
S. *racemosa* 'Goldilocks' (center)

S. *nigra* BLACK BEAUTY (below)

Elephant Ears
Colocasia

C. esculenta 'Illustris,' a Proven Winners Selection (above), C. esculenta with coleus, sweet potato vine and others (right)

$\mathcal{T}$his striking plant will add a tropical look to your, deck or balcony.

Growing
Elephant ears grow well in **light shade** or **full shade**. The potting mix should be **humus rich, slightly acidic** and **moist to wet**. Fertilize every two weeks during the growing season with quarter-strength fertilizer. In cold areas, move elephant ears indoors in winter, or store the tuberous roots in a cool, dry location until spring.

Tips
Planted alone in a moist container or combined with other moisture-lovers, this plant makes a striking addition to any container garden.

Recommended
C. ecsulenta is a tuberous, warm-climate plant that produces a clump of large, heart-shaped leaves. Cultivars with red- or purple-veined to dark purple or bronze foliage are available. **'Black Magic'** has dark purple leaves. **'Fontanesii'** has green leaves with red to purple stems, veins and margins.

Elephant ears are often included in water gardens and can be grown in up to 8" of water. Try them in a large water barrel if you want something other than miniature water lilies.

Also called: taro **Features:** large, dark green to purple leaves **Height:** 2–4' **Spread:** 2–4' **Hardiness:** tender, tuberous perennial grown as an annual

Euonymus

Euonymus

E. fortunei GOLD SPLASH

This group of variable shrubs includes some of the best-suited woody plants for container culture.

Growing

Euonymus prefers **full sun** but tolerates light shade or partial shade. The potting mix should be **moist** and **well drained**. Fertilize monthly during the growing season with quarter-strength fertilizer. In cold areas, move this plant to a sheltered location out of the wind and sun in winter.

Tips

Burning bush has a neat, rounded habit and works well as the center plant in a large mixed container. Wintercreeper euonymus can be allowed to trail over the edge of a container or be trained to

Features: deciduous or evergreen shrub, small tree, groundcover or climber; decorative foliage; good fall color **Height:** 1–10' in containers **Spread:** 1–10' in containers **Hardiness:** zones 3–9

E. alatus FIRE BALL (above)
E. fortunei 'Emerald 'n' Gold' (center)

E. alatus (below)

climb a small trellis. It can also be pruned to form a small shrub or be trained as a topiary plant.

Wintercreeper euonymus is good for winter container gardens and can be planted in the same pots as spring-blooming bulbs. Its low-growing or creeping varieties are especially easy to root as cuttings. Just snip off an 8" section, remove the lowest leaves from the bottom third of the stem and poke the cutting into potting soil.

Recommended

E. alatus (burning bush, winged euonymus) is an attractive, open, mounding, deciduous shrub. It grows far too large to be suitable for a container, but there are several dwarf selections that can be used. '**Compacta**' ('Compactus') is a popular dwarf cultivar. It has dense, compact growth, reaching up to 10' tall and wide, though smaller with pruning and when grown in a container. FIRE BALL ('Select'), a Proven Winners Color Choice Selection, is a hardier selection of 'Compacta' that grows up to 7' tall and wide. It has brilliant red fall color. (Zones 3–8)

E. fortunei (wintercreeper euonymus) as a species is rarely grown in favor of the wide and attractive variety of cultivars. These can be prostrate, climbing or mounding evergreens, often with attractive, variegated foliage. BLONDY ('Interbolwji') has yellow foliage with narrow, irregular, dark green margins. '**Emerald Gaiety**' is a vigorous shrub that sends out long shoots that will attempt to scale any nearby surface. The foliage is bright green with irregular, creamy margins that turn pink in winter. '**Emerald 'n' Gold**' is a bushy selection that has green leaves with wide, gold margins. The foliage turns pinky red during winter and spring. (Zones 5–9)

Euphorbia
Euphorbia

E. polychroma

Once available only with yellow flowers, euphorbia now includes popular hybrid varieties with tiny, repeat-blooming, white or chartreuse flowers and attractive foliage.

Growing

Euphorbia grows well in **full sun** or **light shade**. The potting mix should be **humus rich, moist** and **well drained**. This plant tolerates drought and rarely needs fertilizing. Fertilize once in the growing season, preferably just after

If you are allergic to poinsettias, which are another type of euphorbia, wear gloves when pruning this plant. Some people are sensitive to the milky white sap.

Features: mound-forming perennial; yellow to green, spring to midsummer flowers; decorative foliage; fall color **Height:** 10–36" **Spread:** 12–36" **Hardiness:** zones 4–11

flowering is complete, with quarter- to half-strength fertilizer. In areas that receive frost, move containers to a sheltered location protected from temperature fluctuations in winter. It is evergreen in warmer areas.

Tips

Euphorbia is a neat, rounded plant that is well suited to low-maintenance and drought-tolerant containers.

Recommended

E. amygdaloides 'Efanthia' from Proven Winners has brilliant chartreuse flowers in spring, and its evergreen foliage gets a tinge of burgundy in cool weather. It grows 12–18" tall. **'Helena's Bush,'** the green and white variegated foliage version, grows 10–14" tall. (Zones 4–11).

E. characias **'Glacier Blue'** grows 12–18" tall and bears ice blue, cream-edged foliage and creamy white bracts with a central blue blotch. **'Tasmanian Tiger'** grows 24–36" tall and wide and has gray-green, cream-edged foliage. The flower bracts are pale yellow to creamy white with central green blotches. (Zones 6–10)

E. dulcis (sweet spurge) is a compact, upright plant. The spring flowers and bracts are yellow-green. The dark bronzy green leaves turn red or orange in fall. **'Chameleon'** has purple-red foliage that turns darker purple in fall. (Zones 4–9)

E. griffithii **'Fireglow'** has light green leaves, orange stems and bright orange bracts. **'Fire Charm'** is a more compact selection. (Zones 4–9)

E. hybericifolia **'Diamond Frost'** from Proven Winners looks like an 18" tall fountain of baby's breath, mixes beautifully with other plants and has unusual heat and drought tolerance. (Zones 9–11)

E. x martinii RUDOLPH ('Waleuphrud') grows 18–24" tall and wide and bears tiny, chartreuse green flowers in spring. In the coolness of fall, the plant produces red flower bracts that look like the nose of the famous reindeer. (Zones 6–10)

E. polychroma (*E. epithymoides*; cushion spurge) is a mounding, clump-forming plant. Long-lasting, yellow bracts surround the inconspicuous flowers. The foliage turns shades of purple, red or orange in fall. There are several cultivars available. **'Candy'** has purple-tinged leaves and stems. (Zones 4–9)

E. **'Shorty'** is a mound-forming plant that grows 15–18" tall and wide. It has blue-green foliage whose tips turn rosy red in fall. The flower bracts are bright yellow. (Zones 6–10)

E. dulcis 'Chameleon'

False Cypress
Chamaecyparis

C. pisifera cultivar

The evergreen foliage of false cypress provides winter color as well as solid structure for your container garden.

Growing

False cypress prefers **full sun** along the coast and **partial shade** in hotter areas. In shaded areas, growth may be sparse or thin. The potting mix should be **neutral to acidic, moist** and **well drained**, with lots of compost mixed in. Select a large, stable container so that the plants won't tip over. Fertilize monthly during the growing season with quarter-strength fertilizer.

Avoid severe pruning because new growth will not sprout from old wood. Dry, brown, old leaves can be pulled

Features: narrow, pyramidal, evergreen tree; foliage; habit; cones **Height:** 10"–10' **Spread:** 1–6' **Hardiness:** zones 4–9

C. obtusa 'Nana Gracilis' (above)
C. pisifera cultivar (below)

from the base by hand to tidy up. Dead foliage that appears on older wood may be the result of age or mites. Get rid of it with a blast from the hose. Oils in the foliage of false cypress may be irritating to sensitive skin, so wearing gloves is a good option.

Tips

Tree varieties are used as specimen plants and for hedging. The dwarf and slow-growing cultivars are used in borders and rock gardens and as bonsai. False cypress shrubs can be grown near the house as evergreen specimens in large containers.

Recommended

C. lawsoniana 'Gnome' is a loosely rounded cultivar about 36" tall.

C. nootkatensis is a west coast native with pendulous growth. 'Compacta' is a dense, rounded, compact plant with light green foliage that grows 3–6' tall and wide.

C. obtusa has foliage arranged in fanlike sprays. 'Minima' is a dwarf, mounding cultivar. It grows about 10" tall and spreads 16". 'Nana' is a slow-growing cultivar that reaches 24–36" in height, with a slightly greater spread. 'Nana Gracilis' is upright to broadly pyramidal, grows 3–5' tall and wide and bears dark green foliage. 'Nana Aurea' ('Nana Lutea') is similar to 'Nana Gracilis,' except for its yellow foliage.

C. pisifera 'Nana' is a dwarf cultivar with feathery foliage. It grows into a mound about 12" tall and wide. 'King's Gold' has yellow foliage and grows 18–24" tall and 36" wide. 'Boulevard' has soft, plumey, silver-blue foliage and a pyramidal habit. It turns purple-bronze in winter and grows 6–10' tall and 36" wide. (Zones 4–8)

Fan Flower

Scaevola

Fan flower's intriguing, one-sided flowers add interest to hanging baskets, planters and window boxes.

Growing

Fan flower grows well in **full sun** or **light shade**. The potting mix should be **moist** and **well drained**. Water it regularly because it doesn't like to dry out completely. It does, however, recover quickly from wilting when watered. Fertilize every two weeks with quarter-strength fertilizer. Hardy to 32° F, this perennial is treated as an annual. Take cuttings in late summer and grow indoors for use the following summer.

Tips

Fan flower is popular for hanging baskets and as an edging plant where it can trail down. It is also an attractive filler in mixed containers because it spreads between other plants. Try it with petunias, sweet potato vine, angelonia, verbena and abutilon.

Recommended

S. aemula forms a mound of foliage from which trailing stems emerge. The fan-shaped flowers come in shades of purple, usually with white bases. **'Blue Wonder'** has long, trailing branches, making it ideal for hanging baskets. It can eventually spread 36" or more. **'Saphira'** is a compact variety with deep blue flowers. WHIRLWIND BLUE is a compact plant that bears heat- and fade-resistant, blue flowers. WHIRLWIND WHITE bears white flowers on compact, heat-tolerant plants. **'Jack Russels™ Violet'** from Garden Compass has tiny, non-stop violet flowers with a dense, branching habit and grows 6–8" tall.

S. *aemula* with canna lily, verbena and others

Fan flower is native to Australia and Polynesia. Regular pinching and trimming will keep your fan flower bushy and blooming its best.

Features: decorative, bushy or trailing habit; blue, purple or white, fan-shaped flowers **Height:** up to 8" **Spread:** up to 4' **Hardiness:** tender perennial grown as an annual

Flowering Maple
Abutilon

A. x hybridum

Flowering maple is a vigorous shrub with beautiful flowers and decorative foliage, and it deserves a place in both your garden and your house.

Growing

Flowering maple grows well in **full sun** or **light shade**. The potting mix should be **moist** and **well drained**. Fertilize every two weeks during the growing season with quarter- to half-strength fertilizer. In frosty areas, move flowering maple indoors in winter. Trim it back annually to keep the size manageable.

Tips

Flowering maple makes a stunning specimen, but it is also a lovely companion plant. Plant mounding and trailing annuals around the base of flowering maple to create a pretty display for your front entryway. The blues of salvia and clematis make a nice complement.

Recommended

A. x *hybridum* is a bushy shrub that bears downy, maple-like leaves on woody branches. The single flowers are pendulous and bell-shaped. There are a number of selections available in a variety of colors including peach, white, cream, yellow, orange, red and pink. There are also several selections with variegated foliage. Some of the variegated selections bear very few flowers. **'Goldust'** has salmon-coral flowers. **'Kentish Belle'** bears vibrant orange flowers. **'Nabob'** has crimson red flowers.

A. megapotamimum has arrow-shaped leaves with lantern-shaped flowers on long, graceful branches. **'Marianne'** has a lovely form; **'Variegata'** sports mottled yellow leaves; and **'Victory'** has small, yellow flowers. All are good in hanging baskets.

Also called: Chinese lantern **Features:** tender shrub; maple-like, sometimes variegated foliage; pendulous flowers in shades of yellow, peach, orange, red, pink, cream or white **Height:** 4–5' **Spread:** 24–36" **Hardiness:** zones 8–10

Foamflower

Tiarella

Foamflower's colorful foliage mixes well with other understory plants such as hostas and ferns, and it is great for contrasting and highlighting brightly colored flowers.

Growing

Foamflower prefers **full shade, light shade** or **partial shade** with no afternoon sun. The potting mix should be **moist, slightly acidic** and **well drained**, with lots of compost and/or earthworm castings mixed in. Allow the soil to dry slightly between waterings. Fertilize once a month during the growing season with quarter- to half-strength fertilizer.

Divide in spring. Deadhead to encourage reblooming. Some foamflowers spread by runners, which are easily pulled up to stop excessive spread. If the foliage fades or rusts in summer, cut it partway to the ground, and new growth will emerge.

Tips

Use foamflower as an edging plant or filler plant in your perennial or mixed containers.

Recommended

T. **'Pirates Patch'** is a compact, mounded, slowly creeping plant with large, medium green, slightly lobed foliage centrally marked with dark burgundy. It produces a plethora of pink-tinged, white flowers. The foliage has wonderful reddish purple fall color.

T. **'Skeleton Key'** has white flowers and deeply cut, dark green, glossy foliage with purple tinges along the veins and midrib.

T. hybrid

The starry flowers clustered along the stems look like festive sparklers.

Features: attractive and varied foliage; spring to early-summer, white or pink flowers **Height:** 4–12" **Spread:** 12–24" **Hardiness:** zones 3–8

Fothergilla
Fothergilla

F. gardenii 'Blue Mist'

Fragrant flowers, stunning fall color and interesting, brownish tan stems give fothergilla year-round appeal.

Growing
Fothergilla grows well in **full sun, light shade** or **partial shade** in areas with hot summers. The best flowering and fall color occur in full sun. The potting mix should be **acidic, humus rich, moist** and **well drained**. Add compost or worm castings to the mix. Fertilize with quarter-strength fertilizer every two weeks during the growing season. Move containers to a sheltered location out of the wind and sun in winter.

Tips
Fothergilla forms a striking focal point in mixed containers. Combine it with spring-blooming plants such as tulips for early-season contrast and silver-leaved plants such as dusty miller and licorice plant for fall contrast.

Recommended
F. gardenii (dwarf fothergilla) is a bushy shrub. The dark green leaves turn brilliant, mixed shades of yellow, orange and red in fall. Bottlebrush-shaped flowers are produced in spring and have a delicate honey fragrance. **'Blue Mist'** has blue-green foliage that is pretty in summer, but it doesn't develop brilliant fall color like the species does.

F. major *(large fothergilla) is very similar in appearance to dwarf fothergilla, but it is not as suitable for container culture because it grows at least twice as large.*

Features: bushy shrub; attractive foliage; good fall color; fragrant, white, spring flowers **Height:** 24–36" **Spread:** 24–36" **Hardiness:** zones 4–8

Fuchsia

Fuchsia

F. x hybrida 'Gartenmeister Bonstedt'

Colorful fuchsias were once the province of cool-summer areas. New heat-tolerant varieties allow gardeners in warmer climes to grow these beauties as well.

Growing

Fuchsias grow best in **partial shade** or **light shade**. Fuchsia heat tolerance is improving, but full sun can be too hot for them. The potting mix should be **moist** and **well drained**. Fertilize

Fuchsias bloom on new growth, which will be stimulated by a high-nitrogen plant food.

Features: pink, orange, red, purple or white, often bicolored flowers; attractive foliage
Height: 6"–6' **Spread:** 6–36" **Hardiness:** zones 6–11; tender shrub grown as an annual

F. x hybrida cultivar

bi-weekly during the growing season with half-strength fertilizer. Fuchsias should be deadheaded. Pluck the swollen seedpods from behind the fading petals.

Tender fuchsias can be overwintered indoors in bright—but not burning—light. Make sure they have enough humidity by placing them on a tray of pebbles in water. Many hardy fuchsias will overwinter outside near the coast. Don't prune off the dead branches until you see new growth coming from soil level. Some varieties are ever-blooming in mild areas.

Tips

Upright fuchsias can be used in mixed containers. Pendulous fuchsias are most often used in hanging baskets, but they also look great spilling over the edge of a large container. Hardy fuchsias can be the focal point of large container gardens, but they are slow to get started in spring. Pair them with early-blooming pansies, creeping evergreen euonymus or dwarf rhododendrons and azaleas.

Recommended

F. **Angels' Earrings Series** are from Proven Winners and are very heat and humidity tolerant plants, growing 10–12" tall.

F. x *hybrida* offers dozens of wonderful hybrids. The upright selections grow 18–36" tall, and the pendulous fuchsias grow 6–24" tall. **California Dreamers Series** has heat-tolerant varieties with large blooms and includes '**Bella Rosella**' with pink outer petals and a lavender center; trailing, double-flowered '**Deep Purple**' is a rich purple topped by contrasting white sepals; '**Flamenco Dancer**' has white sepals with a marbled red center; '**Rocket Fire**' has sizzling crimson red blooms; and trailing, double-blooming '**Snowburner**' mixes delicate pink and eye-popping red. All look fantastic in hanging baskets and grow 6–12" high. '**Gartenmeister Bonstedt**' is an upright cultivar that grows about 24" tall and bears tubular, orange-red flowers. The foliage is bronzy red with purple undersides.

F. **magellanica** (hardy fuchsia) is an upright, bushy shrub that grows 4–6' tall and 24–36" wide in containers. It blooms from late spring to the first frost in fall. '**Aurea**' is a low, spreading plant that bears red flowers and yellow-green foliage that can take on purple highlights in fall.

Gaura

Gaura

With its long, graceful flowering stems waving in the breeze, gaura is an excellent addition to your container garden. This repeat bloomer looks like a cloud of small butterflies and is sure to attract welcome attention.

Growing

Gaura favors **full sun**, but some varieties will still bloom in shade. The potting mix should be **well drained**. Although drought tolerant, gaura looks better with regular watering. Flowers bloom and fade progressively along the stem. Go ahead and trim them back in mid-summer to tidy things up and prompt new growth.

Tips

Gaura looks beautiful on its own—try mixing white and pink varieties together. Favorite gaura companions include angelonia, coral bells, African daisy, nemesia and Mexican feather grass.

Recommended

G. lindheimeri is a vase-shaped plant with abundant pink or white flowers born aloft on thin branches. **'Passionate Rainbow'** is a pink-flowered variety with unusual green, white and pink variegated foliage and grows 24–30" tall. **'Sunny Butterflies'** has abundant pink flowers and gray-green, white-edged leaves. It flowers from spring to frost and grows 24" tall. Heat-tolerant **'Crimson Butterflies'** sports attractive dark crimson leaves and hot pink flowers on 8" long stems. This one is compact— only 15" tall. **'Blushing Butterflies'** has dark green leaves and blush pink flowers and grows to 24" tall. All varieties spread about 24".

G. lindheimeri cultivar with weigela, phlox and petunia

Gaura is derived from the Greek word gauros, meaning "superb," "noble" or "proud."

Also called: bee blossom, wand flower
Features: clump-forming perennial; long, branching stems; white, pink or reddish pink flowers **Height:** 15"–4' **Spread:** 12–24" **Hardiness:** zones 6–11

Geranium

Pelargonium

P. peltatum cultivar with lobelia

Geraniums are perhaps the quintessential container plants, and for good reason—they perform exceptionally well in containers. There are a wide variety of geraniums available, and they grow well with many other plants. Try the scented geraniums for their uniquely decorative and wonderfully fragrant foliage as well as for their flowers.

Features: decorative, often colorful foliage; red, pink, violet, orange, salmon, white or purple, summer flowers **Height:** 8–24" **Spread:** 6"–4' **Hardiness:** tender perennial

Growing

Geraniums prefer **full sun** on the coast and **partial shade** inland. The potting mix should be **well drained**. Fertilize with quarter-strength fertilizer every one or two weeks during the growing season. Deadhead to keep geraniums blooming and looking neat, and pinch them back occasionally to keep plants bushy.

Geraniums are perennials that are treated as annuals. They can be kept indoors over winter in a bright room. You can also overwinter geraniums by putting them in a protected, frost-free place and keeping the soil very dry. Begin to water in March and then fertilize in April just before bringing the plants back outdoors after all danger of frost has passed in May. In zones 9–11, treat them as perennials.

Tips

With their brightly colored flowers and decorative foliage, geraniums are very popular for mixed containers, window boxes and hanging baskets. Plant the scented variety near paths and walkways where people can brush against them to release their fragrance.

Recommended

P. capitatum is a compact plant with irregularly shaped, rose-scented leaves. It bears pinkish purple flowers.

P. '**Chocolate Peppermint**' has green leaves with irregular, bronze-purple centers that smell like chocolatey peppermint. The flowers are pink and white.

P. crispum (lemon-scented geranium) forms a compact, low or upright mound of bright green, crinkly, lemon-scented foliage. It bears small, pink flowers in summer. '**Cream Peach**' has green, cream and yellow variegated, peach-scented foliage. '**Variegatum**' ('Variegated Prince Rupert') has ruffled, cream variegated, lemon-scented foliage.

P. x *hortorum* (zonal geranium) is a bushy plant with red, pink, purple, orange or white flowers and frequently banded or multi-colored foliage. The **Fireworks Collection** includes several cultivars with star-shaped flowers in several shades including red and pink. The maple leaf–shaped foliage is colorfully banded. Plants have a compact habit.

P. peltatum (ivy-leaved geranium) has thick, waxy leaves and a trailing habit. It bears loose clusters of colorful flowers. Many cultivars are available.

P. peltatum with portulaca in planter and petunias (above), *P. peltatum* cultivar with jasmine and bacopa (below)

Glory Bush
Tibouchina

T. urvilleana

Glory bush is a wonderful, colorful accent plant that will give a tropical look to your containers.

Growing
Glory bush grows best in **full sun** in a **sheltered** location. The potting mix should be **slightly acidic, moist** and **well drained**. Fertilize every two weeks during the growing season with quarter- to half-strength fertilizer. In cold areas, overwinter in a sunny room or provide adequate frost protection in zone 9. Elsewhere, glory bush requires no special seasonal care.

Tips
Glory bush is useful as a specimen or as an accent in a mixed container. It can be trained into a small tree. Control leginess by trimming after each bloom cycle. The velvety leaves provide an attractive backdrop for red or orange flowers.

Recommended
T. urvilleana is a fast-growing, upright to rounded shrub. The dark green, velvety leaves may have red margins, and older foliage may be marked and spotted yellow, orange and red. Fat, rounded, red-tinged buds open to reveal vivid, royal purple flowers in late spring to late fall.

Also called: princess flower, pleroma, Brazilian spider flower **Features:** bushy, erect to rounded, evergreen shrub; dark green, velvety foliage; purple flowers **Height:** 5–10' **Spread:** 5–10' **Hardiness:** zones 10–11; tender shrub grown as an annual or overwintered indoors

Golden Hakone Grass

Hakonechloa

Golden hakone grass is an attractive, shade-loving grass that provides interest throughout the growing season. It resembles a small bamboo.

Growing

Golden hakone grass grows well in **light shade** or **partial shade**. The potting mix should be **moist** and **well drained**. Fertilize every two weeks during the growing season with quarter- to half-strength fertilizer. Where it is hardy, move the container to a sheltered location out of the wind and sun where it will be protected from temperature fluctuations in winter. Where it is not hardy, it can be cut back and overwintered in an unheated shed or garage.

Tips

With graceful, yellow-striped leaf blades, golden hakone grass is one of the few grasses that grow well in shaded locations. Its texture and color are a good contrast to broad-leaved shade plants such as hosta and lungwort. For best color, avoid deep shade and hot, sunny areas. This grass creates a striking display spilling over the sides of containers. It looks lovely paired with red Japanese maple trees in a large pot.

Recommended

H. macra forms a clump of bright green, arching, grass-like foliage that turns deep pink in fall, then bronze as winter sets in. Several cultivars are available. **'All Gold'** has pure gold leaves and is more upright and spiky in habit. **'Aureola'** has bright yellow foliage with narrow, green streaks; the foliage turns pink in fall.

H. macra 'Aureola' with ligularia, begonia and lysimachia

This ornamental grass is native to Japan, where it grows on mountainsides and cliffs, often near streams and other water sources.

Also called: Japanese forest grass **Features:** perennial grass; arching habit; fall color **Height:** 12–24" **Spread:** 12–24" **Hardiness:** zones 5–8

Golden Marguerite
Anthemis

A. tinctoria

Shear plants back as flowering finishes to encourage fresh growth and a second flush of flowers.

Also called: marguerite daisy **Features:** mounding or spreading perennial; yellow, orange or cream, daisy-like, summer flowers; finely divided or feathery foliage **Height:** 8–36" **Spread:** 12–36" **Hardiness:** zones 3–9

Pretty, daisy-like flowers almost completely cover the fine, feathery foliage when these plants are in bloom.

Growing

Golden marguerite grows best in **full sun**. The potting mix should be **well drained**. This plant tolerates drought. Fertilize monthly during the growing season with quarter-strength fertilizer. Move hardy plants to a sheltered location in winter. Where they are not hardy, store containers in a shed or garage in winter.

Tips

Golden marguerite can be planted alone in specimen containers and is also a cheerful addition to mixed containers. The daisy-like flowers have a warm, welcoming appearance that makes them a good choice for containers placed near an entryway.

Recommended

A. marshalliana (marshall chamomile) is a low, mound-forming plant. Its finely divided leaves are covered in long, silvery hairs. Bright golden yellow flowers are borne in summer.

A. punctata subsp. *cupaniana* forms a low mat of silvery gray foliage. It bears yellow-centered, white flowers in early summer. (Zones 6–8)

A. tinctoria (golden marguerite) forms a mounded clump of foliage that is completely covered in bright or pale yellow, daisy-like flowers in summer. 'Charme' is a compact plant that grows 12–16" tall and 12" wide with bright yellow flowers. 'Grallach Gold' bears bright golden yellow flowers. 'Moonlight' bears large, buttery or pale yellow flowers.

Hardy Geranium
Geranium

G. JOLLY BEE, a Proven Winners Selection

Hardy geraniums are available in a huge range of heights and colors, at least some of which are sure to suit your container garden needs.

Growing

Hardy geraniums prefer **partial shade** or **light shade** but tolerate full sun. The potting mix should be **well drained**. Fertilize every two weeks during the growing season with quarter-strength fertilizer. In cold areas, move containers to a sheltered location protected from temperature fluctuations in winter. Be prepared to prune this robust plant, or it will overtake the other plants in the pot.

Also called: cranesbill **Features:** clump- or mound-forming perennial; dense, often deeply divided foliage; white, red, pink, purple or blue, summer flowers **Height:** 6–36" **Spread:** 12–36" **Hardiness:** zones 3–11

G. 'Johnson's Blue' (above)
G. *pratense* 'Plenum Violaceum' (below)

Tips

These long-flowering plants are great in mixed containers. The simple flowers aren't exceptionally showy, but their constant presence is appreciated as other flowers come and go.

Recommended

G. 'Johnson's Blue' forms a spreading mat of foliage. Bright blue flowers are borne over a long period in summer.

G. JOLLY BEE is a vigorous, mounding plant with large, violet-blue flowers that bloom for an extended period in summer and have orange to red fall color.

G. *macrorrhizum* (bigroot cranesbill) forms a spreading mound of fragrant foliage. This plant is quite drought tolerant. Flowers in variable shades of pink are borne in spring and early summer.

G. x *oxonianum* is a vigorous, mound-forming plant with attractive, evergreen foliage. It bears pink flowers from spring to fall.

G. *pratense* (meadow cranesbill) forms an upright clump and bears clusters of white, blue or light purple flowers for a short period in early summer. It self-seeds freely. **'Plenum Violaceum'** bears purple, double flowers for a longer period than the species.

G. *sanguineum* (bloody cranesbill, bloodred cranesbill) forms a dense, mounding clump and bears bright magenta flowers mostly in early summer and sporadically until fall. **'Elsbeth'** has light pink flowers with dark pink veins and bright red fall foliage. **'Shepherd's Warning'** grows 6" tall and bears rosy pink flowers. **Var. *striatum*** tolerates heat and drought. It has pale pink blooms with blood red veins.

Hebe
Hebe

H. speciosa 'Tricolor'

ebes are attractive, low-mainte-nance shrubs that are wonderful container garden plants.

Growing
Hebes grow well in **full sun** or **partial shade** in a **sheltered** location. The potting mix should be **neutral to alkaline, moist** and **very well drained**. Fertilize once a month during the growing season with quarter- to half-strength fertilizer. Hebes tolerate urban pollution.

Many hebes work year-round in the garden. In frost areas, move them to a cool, bright room indoors in winter. Plants may be damaged by early fall or late spring frost.

Most hebes need little or no pruning. Large-leaved hebes benefit from removing the spent flower spikes. Leggy or neglected plants, or plants damaged by a hard winter, can be cut back hard to 6–12" above the soil in spring.

Tips
Hebes can be planted with annuals and perennials in mixed containers and are also excellent as specimens. They make wonderful evergreen shrubs for a mixed container that you want to look good even in winter.

Features: tender, mound-forming, evergreen shrub; dense, attractive foliage; purple, red, pink, blue or white, fragrant flowers **Height:** 8"–5' **Spread:** 2–5' **Hardiness:** zones 8–11

H. 'Veronica Lake' (above), H. speciosa (below)

Recommended

H. buxifolia (box-leaf hebe) grows 3–4' tall and wide. It has small, bright green, boxwood-like foliage and bears small spikes of white flowers in early summer.

H. cupressoides is a whipcord hebe that forms a dense, upright mound of small, scale-like foliage that closely resembles cypress foliage. The plant grows 3–4' tall and wide and bears lilac flowers that fade to white. **'Boughton Dome'** forms a dense mound 12" tall and 24" wide.

H. pinguifolia 'Pagei' is a low-growing groundcover that roots at the nodes. It grows 8–12" tall and 4–5' wide, bearing small, blue-gray leaves and white, summer flowers.

H. rakaiensis 'Golden Dome' is an attractive choice for cottage gardens, with white flower spikes and glossy, green foliage that turns yellow in winter. This compact variety grows 24" tall and wide.

H. 'Red Edge' is a compact plant that bears blue-green foliage with thin, red margins. The leaves are tinged red when young. It grows about 18" tall and 24" wide, producing lilac blooms that fade to white in summer.

Generally, small-leaved hebes are hardier than large-leaved hebes.

Heliotrope
Heliotropium

Heliotrope's big clusters of fragrant flowers on bushy plants have renewed the popularity of this old-fashioned favorite.

Growing

Heliotrope grows best in **full sun** near the coast and **partial shade** in warmer areas. The potting mix should be **humus rich, moist** and **well drained**. Fertilize once a month during the growing season with quarter-strength fertilizer. Deadhead for repeat blooms. Plants can be treated as houseplants in winter; keep them in a cool and sunny location indoors. Cut back in spring for bushier plants. Heliotrope is very attractive to slugs and snails. Pick them off as soon as you spot them.

Tips

Heliotrope is ideal for growing in containers placed where the wonderful scent of the flowers can be enjoyed. Combine purple-flowered heliotrope with yellow- or white-flowered plants and plants with burgundy foliage for striking color contrasts. When mixing it with other plants, don't crowd heliotrope or it may get powdery mildew.

Recommended

H. arborescens is a low, bushy shrub that bears large clusters of sweet-scented, purple flowers all summer. Some new cultivars are not as strongly scented as the species. **'Black Beauty'** bears deep purple, fragrant flowers. **'Blue Wonder'** is a compact plant with heavily scented, dark purple flowers. **'Nagano'** from Proven Winners has fragrant, vanilla-scented blossoms on a vigorous, heat-tolerant plant with dark green foliage and grows 10–14" tall.

H. arborescens ATLANTIS with angelonia, lobelia, sweet flag, licorice plant and sage

Also called: cherry pie plant **Features:** bushy habit; purple or white, fragrant flowers; attractive foliage **Height:** 8–24" **Spread:** 12–24" **Hardiness:** zones 10–11; tender shrub grown as an annual

Hens and Chicks

Sempervivum

S. tectorum with phormium

ens and chicks are easy to grow. They need little care other than a very well-drained soil and a light sprinkle of water during extended dry periods.

Also called: houseleek **Features:** rosette-forming, succulent perennial; red, yellow, white or purple flowers **Height:** 2–6"
Spread: 12" or more **Hardiness:** zones 3–8

Growing

Hens and chicks grow well in **full sun** or **partial shade**. The potting mix should be **very well drained**. Add fine gravel or grit to the mix to provide adequate drainage. Fertilize once or twice during the growing season with quarter-strength fertilizer.

Tips

These plants can be used in shallow troughs and make interesting center-pieces on patio and picnic tables. They can also be combined with other drought-tolerant plants, such as sedum and yarrow, in mixed containers. Creative container gardeners enjoy growing these succulents in old shoes, boots, metal toy dump trucks and just about any other container with drainage holes.

Recommended

S. tectorum is one of the most commonly grown hens and chicks of the many species, cultivars and hybrids available. It forms a low-growing mat of fleshy-leaved rosettes. Small, new rosettes are quickly produced and grow and multiply to fill almost any space. Flowers may be produced in summer. 'Atropurpureum' has dark reddish purple leaves. 'Limelight' has yellow-green, pink-tipped foliage. 'Pacific Hawk' has dark red leaves that are edged with silvery hairs.

S. arachnoideum (cobweb houseleek) is identical to *S. tectorum* except that the tips of the leaves are entwined with hairy fibers, giving the appearance of cobwebs. This plant may need protection during wet weather.

Hosta

Hosta

H. cultivar with others

If you have a covered entryway so shaded that few flowers will bloom, place a pair of potted hostas on either side of the door for a dramatic and refreshing welcome.

Growing

Hostas prefer **light shade** or **partial shade** but will grow in full shade. Some will tolerate full sun. By growing hostas in containers, you can move them to receive the appropriate amount of sun.

The potting mix should be **moist** and **well drained**. Fertilize monthly during the growing season with half-strength fertilizer. If the temperature drops below 30° F, move containers to a

Also called: plantain lily **Features:** clump-forming perennial; decorative foliage in shades of green or variegated with yellow or cream; late-summer or fall, mauve, purple or white flowers **Height:** 1–4' **Spread:** 18–36" **Hardiness:** zones 3–8

H. fortuneii 'Francee' (above), *H. cultivar* (center)

H. cultivar with coral bells and barberry (below)

sheltered location in winter. Hostas are slug and snail magnets, so be on the lookout for these pests.

Hostas can grow in the same pot for many years without needing a transplant, but as the roots become more crowded, the leaves will become smaller and the plants will require more water.

Tips

Hostas are wonderful woodland plants and look very attractive when combined with ferns and other fine-textured plants, especially in dark or rustic containers. Combine a variety of hostas or mix them with other plants.

Recommended

Hostas have been subjected to a great deal of crossbreeding and hybridizing, resulting in hundreds of cultivars. There are almost endless variations in hosta foliage; swirls, stripes, puckers and ribs enhance the leaves' various sizes, shapes and colors. **'Baby Bunting'** is a popular cultivar with dark green to slightly bluish green, heart-shaped leaves and light purple flowers. **'Fragrant Bouquet'** has bright green leaves with creamy yellow margins and very fragrant, white flowers. **'Gold Standard'** is a hosta fancier's favorite, bearing bright yellow leaves with narrow, green margins. **'Guacamole'** has chartreuse leaves with dark green margins and fragrant, white flowers. **'June'** has bright yellow leaves with blue-green margins and light purple flowers. **'Pandora's Box'** forms a compact mound of creamy leaves with irregular, green margins and bears light purple flowers. **'Tardiflora'** forms an attractive, small mound of dark green leaves and bears lots of light purple flowers in fall.

Hydrangea
Hydrangea

Proven Winners Selection *H. paniculata* LIMELIGHT

From rounded shrubs and small trees to climbing vines, hydrangeas offer a wealth of possibilities. Watch for new dwarf varieties that are perfect for containers.

Growing

Hydrangeas grow well in **full sun** on the coast and **partial shade** elsewhere; some species tolerate full shade. These plants perform best in cool, moist conditions, and some shade will reduce leaf and flower scorch in hotter gardens. The potting mix should be **humus rich, moist** and **well drained**. Fertilize monthly during the growing season with quarter- to half-strength fertilizer.

Features: mounding, spreading or climbing, deciduous shrub or tree; clusters of white, pink, blue, purple or red flowers in summer; attractive foliage, sometimes with good fall color; some with exfoliating bark **Height:** 1–10' **Spread:** 3–10' **Hardiness:** zones 3–9

H. macrophylla

Move containers to a sheltered location out of the wind and sun in winter.

Tips

Hydrangeas can really brighten up your mixed containers with their large flower clusters. Shrubby forms can be grown alone or combined with other plants. Tree forms are small enough to grow in containers but large enough to offer a good vertical accent. Climbing hydrangea can be used to create a beautiful display against a wall or over the edge of a balcony.

Recommended

H. anomala subsp. *petiolaris* (climbing hydrangea) is an elegant climbing plant with dark green, glossy leaves. It bears clusters of lacy-looking flowers in mid-summer. Unlike most hydrangeas, this climber needs at least half a day of sun to bloom. (Zones 4–8)

H. arborescens 'Annabelle' (Annabelle hydrangea) is a rounded shrub that bears large clusters of white flowers, even in shady conditions.

H. macrophylla (bigleaf hydrangea) is a rounded shrub that bears flowers in shades of pink, red, blue or purple from mid- to late summer. The acidity of the planting mix affects the color of the blooms. The pH of most mixes will yield pink flowers. Make the soil more acidic if you want blue flowers. ENDLESS SUMMER bears deep pink, mophead flower clusters over a long season on current and prior-year growth. It can be pruned any time and not suffer from a lack of flowers the following year. It is quite tolerant of cold winters and late spring frosts (zones 5–8). The **Dwarf Cityline Hydrangea Collection** from Proven Winners includes **'Berlin,'** a large-flowered, clear pink, mildew-resistant beauty that tops out at 32" tall and 3–4' wide; **'Paris,'** with dark red blooms maturing to green, also extremely resistant to mildew; and **'Venice,'** with full-size fuchsia blooms and a tiny stature of 12–36" tall (zones 5–9). **'Mini Penny'** from Monrovia blooms repeatedly in pink and blue from summer to frost on compact bushes that grow 24–36" tall and 3–4' wide (zones 6–9).

H. quercifolia (oakleaf hydrangea) is a mound-forming shrub with attractive, cinnamon brown, exfoliating bark. Its beautiful large, leathery leaves are lobed like an oak's and turn bronze to bright red in fall. It bears conical clusters of sterile as well as fertile flowers. (Zones 4–8)

Hyssop
Agastache

This perennial is a favorite with hummingbirds, butterflies, other pollinators—and gardeners.

Growing

Hyssop grows well in **full sun** or **partial shade**. The potting mix should be **well drained**. Fertilize every two weeks during the growing season with quarter-strength fertilizer. Deadheading will keep plants neat and encourage continued blooming. Although hyssop is somewhat tolerant of low water conditions, it looks better with regular water. In cold regions, overwinter tender selections indoors or replace each year. Hardy selections can be kept in a sheltered spot outdoors in winter.

Tips

These bushy plants make good companions in mixed containers. Combine them with lavender, scented-leaf geranium, lilac and thyme for a fragrance-themed container that is sure to attract pollinators to your garden.

Recommended

A. aurantiaca is a bushy, upright plant with gray-green, mint-scented leaves. It bears spikes of orange-pink flowers in summer. **'Apricot Sprite'** bears lots of apricot orange flowers. (Zones 7–10)

A. **'Firebird'** has irregular, bronzy maroon markings on its leaves and bears spikes of coppery orange flowers in summer. (Zones 6–10)

A. foeniculum (anise hyssop) is a bushy, upright, anise-scented perennial with slightly downy leaves and dense spikes of lilac blue flowers. **'Snow Spike'** has white flowers.

A. foeniculum

A. rupestris **'Acapulco Salmon & Pink'** from High Country Gardens has bicolored, tubular blossoms in pink and orange. **'Orange Flare'** from the same breeder is a fragrant variety with gray foliage and deep orange flowers.

Also called: hummingbird mint **Features:** bushy, upright perennial; mint or licorice-scented foliage; pink, purple, purple-blue or orange flowers **Height:** 12–36" **Spread:** 12–36" **Hardiness:** zones 2–10

Impatiens
Impatiens

I. walleriana with baby tears and vinca

Impatiens, with their brightly colored flowers, are just as valuable in shady containers as they are in shady ground-based gardens.

Growing

Impatiens do best in **partial shade** or **light shade** but tolerate full shade or, if kept moist, full sun. New Guinea impatiens are best adapted to sunny locations, but the foliage may still scorch in

Features: bushy or spreading habit; flowers in shades of purple, red, burgundy, pink, orange, salmon, apricot, yellow or white, or bicolored **Height:** 6–21" **Spread:** 8–24" **Hardiness:** tender annual

hot afternoon sun. The potting mix should be **humus rich, moist** and **well drained**. Do not let impatiens dry out. Mix in some compost or earthworm castings. Fertilize every two weeks with quarter-strength fertilizer.

Tips

These bushy or spreading plants make great colorful fillers in shady containers. Impatiens will contrast or complement the other plants in your containers. Combine impatiens with begonia and lobelia in shades of white and yellow to light up a deeply shaded area. They also look great with bright-colored coleus and trailing sweet potato vine.

Recommended

I. auricoma are relatively new impatiens in a fresh color—yellow. With orchid-like flowers held above dark green foliage, **'Jungle Gold'** is recommended for containers because it takes slightly less water and more shade than traditional impatiens and grows 15–18" tall. Full sun reduces flowering.

I. hawkeri (New Guinea Group, New Guinea impatiens) are bushy plants with glossy, dark green foliage that is often variegated with a yellow stripe down the center. The flowers come in shades of red, orange, pink, purple or white. Cultivars are available.

I. walleriana (busy Lizzie) is a bushy, spreading plant with glossy leaves in shades of light through dark green or bronze. The flowers come in shades of purple, red, burgundy, pink, orange, salmon, apricot, yellow or white, or bicolored. Many cultivars are available. **'Firefly'** has dark green leaves and tiny blossoms.

Iris

Iris

Irises are valuable both for their strap-like foliage and their beautiful, colorful flowers.

Growing

Irises grow best in **full sun** but tolerate partial shade or light shade. The potting mix should be **moist** and **well drained**, though several species tolerate dry conditions. Fertilize monthly during the growing season with quarter-strength fertilizer. In cold weather regions, move containers to a sheltered location out of the wind and sun in winter.

Tips

Irises provide a wonderful strong, vertical accent. Several species grow in wet soil and can be combined with other moisture-lovers such as cardinal flower and elephant ears for a bog-themed container. There are iris flowers in almost every imaginable shade, and these can be used to create complementary or contrasting combinations in mixed containers.

Recommended

I. ensata (Japanese iris) is a water-loving species that bears blue, purple, pink or white flowers in early to midsummer.

I. germanica **hybrids** (German iris, bearded iris) are drought-tolerant plants that bear the most decorative flowers in every imaginable color.

I. pallida (sweet iris, variegated iris) is a drought-tolerant, purple-flowered species that is rarely grown, but its variegated cultivars are a useful addition to mixed containers. '**Argentea Variegata**' has cream-and-green-striped foliage. '**Aurea Variegata**' has yellow-and-green-striped foliage.

Iris with others

Features: clump-forming, rhizomatous perennial; narrow or broad, strap-like, possibly variegated foliage; summer flowers in every shade of the rainbow **Height:** 1–4' **Spread:** 8–36" **Hardiness:** zones 2–8

I. pseudacorus (yellow flag iris) is a moisture-loving species with narrow foliage and bright yellow, brown- or purple-marked flowers in mid- and late summer.

I. sibirica (Siberian iris) likes a moist but well-drained soil. It bears purple flowers in early summer, though cultivars with pink, blue, white, yellow or red flowers are available.

I. versicolor (blue flag iris) is a moisture-loving species that bears flowers in varied shades of purple in early summer.

Irises are steeped in history and lore. The name Iris *comes from the Greek messenger to the gods, who traveled using the rainbow as a bridge.*

I. germanica 'Stepping Out' (above), *I. pseudacorus* (below)

Japanese Painted Fern

Athyrium

A. niponicum 'Silver Falls'

Delicate, decorative and well behaved: *Athyrium* is one of the few fern genera really suitable for container culture.

Growing

A slow grower, this fern does well in **full shade, partial shade** or **light shade**. The potting mix should be **acidic** and **moist**. Fertilize every two weeks during the growing season with quarter-strength fertilizer. It will need some protection in

The demand for these wonderful ferns will certainly encourage enthusiastic breeders to create more varieties.

Features: deciduous, perennial fern; decorative foliage **Height:** 1–4' **Spread:** 1–4' **Hardiness:** zones 4–8

A. niponicum var. pictum with iris, heucherella and others (above), A. felix-femina (below)

winter. Cover it if it will be left out-doors, or move it to a sheltered location.

Tips

These ferns make an attractive addition to almost any mixed planter. Combine hosta, coral bells, Annabelle hydrangea and either *Athyrium* species in a large planter for a shaded location. Try com-bining the gray foliage of dusty miller or licorice plant with pots of Japanese painted fern to bring out the silver high-lights on the leaves. This colorful fern also looks great in a sleek metallic pot for a contemporary container garden.

Recommended

A. felix-femina (lady fern) forms a dense clump of lacy fronds. The appear-ance can be quite variable, as the leaflets on the fronds and the fronds themselves are prone to dividing, giving the plants a more lacy appearance or sometimes even a dense, ball-like appearance. It varies in size from dwarfs that grow 12" tall and wide to larger plants that can grow 2–4' tall and wide. Interesting cul-tivars include **'Dre's Dagger,'** with nar-row leaflets arranged in four rows around each frond, and **'Encourage,'** whose leaflets are divided at the tips, giving a frilly or fan-like appearance to the outer edges of each frond. Somewhat harder to find is **'Acrocladon,'** whose fronds subdivide so often that the fern appears to be a small, dense ball of foliage.

A. niponicum var. pictum (Japanese painted fern) is a low, creeping fern with reddish to burgundy stems and a silvery metallic sheen to the bronzy fronds. Several cultivars have been developed with varied frond colors. **'Burgundy Lace'** has pinkish purple fronds with a metallic sheen. **'Pewter Lace'** has pew-ter-silver fronds with purple highlights. **'Ruby Red'** has a ruffled look, and the dark red fronds have bright silver edges.

Jasmine
Jasminum

*P*lant a delightfully scented jasmine in a large pot near the entrance to your home or on your patio and enjoy the wonderful fragrance. There are many varieties with different requirements for all different climate conditions.

Growing

Jasmine grows best in **full sun** or **partial shade**. The potting mix should be **moist** and **well drained**. Fertilize lightly in spring. Water consistently during summer but lessen frequency in winter. Pinch and prune to control the shape and growth. Some varieties need cold to initiate bloom; others only bloom during long, warm summers.

Tips

Consider whether you want your jasmine to spread or climb. Choose a large container if you want your plant to cascade and select a support if you want it to be vertical.

Recommended

J. nitidum 'Angelwing' has 1" wide, highly fragrant, pinwheel-shaped, white flowers with purple undersides on glossy, green leaves. It can grow 10–20' tall but responds well to hard pruning. Hardy to 25° F, it blooms most successfully in areas that have a long, warm growing season.

J. officinale 'Hardy Jasmine' is a vigorous climber that needs cold (to freezing and below) to bloom and is hardy to zone 7 or zone 6 when sheltered. It grows 2–4' tall in a container and blooms spring, summer and fall.

J. polyanthem has many scented, white flowers and green leaves variegated with

J. officinale

creamy yellow and white. Hardy to zone 8, it blooms in winter in areas where the temperature falls to 35° F. It grows 12–36" tall in a container.

Features: scented or unscented, trailing evergreen or deciduous shrub or vine
Height: 2–10' in containers **Spread:** 3–6'
Hardiness: zones 6–11

Kalanchoe

Kalanchoe

K. blossfeldiana

alanchoe is an extremely varied group of plants. There are fuzzy ones, waxy ones, cascading ones and upright ones; some have decorative foliage, others are grown strictly for flowers.

Growing

Kalanchoes grow best in **light shade** or **partial shade** with protection from the hot afternoon sun. The potting mix should be **well drained**. Fertilize monthly during the growing season with half-strength fertilizer. Some are hardy outdoors in winter with protection. Others can be moved indoors and

treated as houseplants at the end of summer.

Tips

Kalanchoes are interesting accent plants that add a touch of the unusual to your mixed containers. Their drought tolerance makes them useful for gardeners who occasionally forget to water.

Recommended

K. blossfeldiana (flaming katy) has rounded, fleshy leaves with scalloped edges. The flowers are borne in large clusters in colors such as yellow, peach, red, white or pink.

K. tomentosa (panda plant, pussy ears) has gray-green leaves covered in short, silvery hairs. The tips and margins are marked with brown.

Features: bushy, upright habit; glossy or fuzzy, succulent foliage; colorful flowers
Height: 6–18" **Spread:** 10–18" **Hardiness:** tender perennial grown as an annual

Lady's Mantle
Alchemilla

Few other perennials look as captivating as lady's mantle with droplets of morning dew clinging like shimmering pearls to its velvety leaves.

Growing

Lady's mantle grows well in **light shade** or **partial shade** with protection from the afternoon sun. Hot locations and excessive sun will scorch the leaves. The potting mix should be **humus rich, moist** and **well drained**. Fertilize every two weeks during the growing season with quarter-strength fertilizer. Leaves can be sheared back in summer if they begin to look tired and heat stressed; new leaves will emerge. In cold winter areas, move containers to a sheltered location where they will be protected from temperature fluctuations.

Tips

Lady's mantle is ideal for mixed containers, where it has a visually softening effect. Combine it with yellow- and purple-flowered annuals for an elegant, contrasting combination. Enjoy the flowers from late spring to early summer.

Recommended

A. alpina (alpine lady's mantle) is a low-growing plant that reaches 3–5" tall and spreads about 20". Clusters of tiny, yellow flowers are borne in summer.

A. mollis (common lady's mantle) forms a mound of soft, rounded foliage and produces sprays of frothy-looking, yellowish green flowers in early summer. It grows 8–18" tall and spreads about 24".

A. mollis

The chartreuse yellow flower sprays make interesting substitutes for baby's breath in fresh and dried arrangements.

Features: mound-forming perennial; attractive, downy foliage; yellow or yellow-green, summer and early fall flowers **Height:** 2–18" **Spread:** 18–24" **Hardiness:** zones 3–8

Lamium

Lamium

L. maculatum 'White Nancy' with others

Lamium is usually quite invasive in the ground. Growing it in containers keeps it from spreading out of control.

Features: spreading or trailing perennial; decorative, variegated foliage; pink, white, yellow or purple, small, summer flowers
Height: 6–12" **Spread:** 12–24" **Hardiness:** zones 2–8

These plants, with their striped, dotted or banded, silver and green foliage, provide a summer-long attraction and thrive on the barest necessities of life.

Growing

Lamium grows well in **light shade** or **partial shade** with protection from the hot afternoon sun. The potting mix should be **moist** and **well drained**. Fertilize no more than once a month during the growing season with quarter-strength fertilizer. Move containers to a sheltered location in winter where they will be protected from temperature fluctuations.

Tips

Lamium is a stunning foliage plant, and it makes a fantastic filler in mixed containers. It will trail over the edges of containers. Try it with other colorful foliage plants such as foamflower, coral bells and any grasses.

Recovmmended

L. galeobdolon (*Lamiastrum galeobdolon*; yellow archangel, false lamium) is a mounding, spreading plant with silver-marked leaves and short spikes of yellow flowers in summer. This is a very invasive evergreen perennial in shaded gardens. Don't let it escape from the pot, or it could root and smother your house and garden. **'Florentium'** ('Variegatum') is a low-growing cultivar with silvery leaves edged in green. **'Hermann's Pride'** forms a dense mat of white-speckled leaves. **'Silver Angel'** is a spreading plant with silvery foliage. (Zones 3–8)

L. maculatum (spotted dead nettle) is a low-growing, spreading plant with green leaves with white or silvery markings. It bears short spikes of pink, white or mauve flowers in summer. **'Anne Greenaway'** has silver, green and yellow variegated leaves and lavender flowers. **'Aureum'** has variegated chartreuse and silver foliage and pink flowers. **'Beacon Silver'** has silvery leaves with dark green margins and pink flowers. **'Orchid Frost'** has silvery foliage edged in blue-green and bears deep pink blooms. **'White Nancy,'** with silvery white foliage and white flowers, and **'Golden Anniversary,'** with purple flowers and variegated green foliage, are both Proven Winners Selections.

L. galeobdolon 'Florentium' with others (above)
L. maculatum 'Beacon Silver' with impatiens (below)

Lantana

Lantana

L. camara 'Tropical Fruit' from Proven Winners

Lantana is a cheerful bloomer over long seasons with little water and lots of sun. Both mounding and trailing varieties are available.

Growing
Lantana likes **full sun** and may get mildew if grown in shade. The potting mix should be **fertile, moist** and **well drained**. Once established, it thrives on infrequent, deep watering. Feed every

Lantana leaves can be toxic to pets, according to the U.S. Humane Society.

Features: spreading or trailing perennial; tiny clusters of bright flowers **Height:** 30–36" **Spread:** 18–24" **Hardiness:** zones 9–11; grown as an annual where not hardy

two weeks with quarter-strength fertilizer. Too much water or fertilizer will reduce blooms. If berries form, trim them back to get more flowers.

Tips
Lantana mixes well with million bells, coleus, lobelia, petunia and many others. Try it in a hanging basket, where the occasional lack of water will not harm it.

Recommended
***L. camara* hybrids** such as the **Patriot Series** from Proven Winners bloom continuously in mild winter areas. Mounding **'Desert Sunset'** features flowers in yellow, gold, cantaloupe, peach and deep pink, all on the same plant.

Lavender

Lavandula

Lavender is a beautiful, aromatic plant that is a welcome addition to sunny container gardens.

Growing

Lavender grows best in **full sun**. The potting mix should be **alkaline** and **well drained**. Select a large pot to accommodate this plant's room system. Established plants tolerate heat and drought. Mulch with white oyster shells, white pebbles or 2" of sand to help reflect heat and light onto these sun-loving perennials. In cold winter areas, move containers to a sheltered location and cover them, or move them to an unheated shed or garage. Prune lavender in early spring to about two-thirds of its size.

Tips

Lavender makes a good shrubby addition to mixed containers. Good companions for it include thyme, sedum and rosemary.

Recommended

L. angustifolia (English lavender) is an aromatic, bushy shrub often treated as a perennial. From midsummer to fall, it bears spikes of small flowers in varied shades of purple. **'Hidcote'** ('Hidcote Blue') bears spikes of deep purple flowers. **'Jean Davis'** is a compact cultivar with spikes of pale pink flowers. **'Lady'** bears purple flowers and can be grown from seed to flower the first summer.

L. x intermedia is a rounded shrub with aromatic, gray-green leaves and spikes of blue or purple flowers held on long stems.

L. stoechas (Spanish lavender) is a compact, bushy shrub with gray-green leaves and dark purple flower spikes. **'Kew Red'** bears bright pink flowers with light pink bracts (zone 8). **'Lemon Leigh'**

L. angustifolia

from Monrovia has prolific, unusual yellow and chartreuse flowers. New varieties from Proven Winners include the **Ooh La Lavender Series** in burgundy and pink. These fragrant plants will survive temperatures below 15° F. **'Otto Quast'** has sturdy, purple bracts and will continue blooming following light frosts.

Features: bushy, woody shrub; narrow, gray-green leaves; purple, pink or blue, midsummer to fall flowers **Height:** 8–24" **Spread:** 12–24" **Hardiness:** zones 5–8

Licorice Plant

Helichrysum

H. petiolare 'Petite Licorice' with dusty miller

This plant is a good indicator plant for hanging baskets. When you see licorice plant wilting, it is time to get out the hose or watering can.

Features: bushy or trailing habit; downy, gray-green, silvery, yellow or cream and green variegated foliage **Height:** 6–24" **Spread:** 1–4' **Hardiness:** tender shrub or perennial grown as an annual

The silvery sheen of licorice plant, caused by a fine, soft pubescence on its leaves, makes it a perfect complement for many other plants.

Growing

Licorice plant prefers **full sun**. The potting mix should be **neutral to alkaline** and **well drained**. Be careful not to overwater; licorice plant wilts if the soil dries out but revives quickly once watered. It is easy to start more plants from cuttings in fall, giving you a supply of new plants for the following spring. Once they have rooted, keep the young plants in a cool, bright room during winter.

Tips

Include licorice plant in your hanging baskets and container plantings, and the trailing growth will quickly fill in and provide a soft, silvery setting for the colorful flowers of other plants as it cascades over the edges.

Recommended

H. petiolare is a trailing plant with fuzzy, gray-green leaves. The cultivars are more common than the species. The gray-leaved varieties grow faster than the variegated and green-leaved varieties. '**Crispum**' has small leaves with rippled edges. '**Lemon Licorice**' has yellow-green foliage. '**Licorice Splash**' has gray-green leaves with irregular, creamy margins. '**Limelight**' has bright lime green leaves. '**Petite Licorice**' is a compact selection with small, gray-green leaves. '**Silver**' has gray-green leaves covered in a silvery white down. '**White Licorice**' has silvery white foliage.

Lilac

Syringa

S. x *hyacinthiflora* 'Evangeline'

Even for container gardeners, the hardest thing about growing lilacs is choosing from the many species and hundreds of cultivars available. Many need chilly weather for best performance, but some newer varieties will also bloom in warmer areas.

Growing

Lilacs grow best in **full sun** or **light shade** in warmer areas. The potting mix

Lilacs are frost-loving shrubs that bloom very well in certain cooler areas. Rainy weather makes lilacs more susceptible to leaf blights.

Features: rounded or suckering, deciduous shrub or small tree; attractive, late-spring to midsummer flowers **Height:** 3–15' **Spread:** 3–15' **Hardiness:** zones 3–9

S. x *hyacinthiflora* 'Maiden's Blush'(above),
S. *meyeri* 'Palibin'(below)

should be **humus rich, well drained** and **alkaline.** Fertilize monthly during the growing season with quarter-strength fertilizer. Give them space to avoid powdery mildew. Control growth by pinching; heavy trimming will reduce bloom the following year. Lilacs are among the hardiest of plants. Move containers to a location out of the sun and wind, and they should make it through just about anything winter can throw at them.

Tips

Lilacs make lovely vertical accents and are good structural plants for large containers. Most can be trained into a tree form and can be grown in a container for several years before they become too large and need to be transplanted into a garden.

Recommended

S. x *hyacinthiflora* hybrids are hardy, upright, disease-resistant shrubs that spread with age. They bear clusters of fragrant flowers in mid- to late spring. The leaves turn reddish purple in fall.

S. *meyeri* is a compact, rounded shrub that bears pink or lavender, fragrant flowers. **'Palibin'** is a slow-growing cultivar with pinkish purple flowers. **'Tinkerbelle'** bears deep pink flowers.

S. *patula* 'Miss Kim' is a vigorous, compact lilac with pale purple flower buds that open lavender blue. It has attractive, dark green foliage.

S. *vulgaris* includes several low-chill varieties. **'Angel White'** has white, mildly fragrant flowers and grows 8–10' tall. Sweet-scented **'Blue Skies'** is hardy to zone 9 and has light lavender flowers and attractive green foliage. **'Lavender Lady'** has good fragrance and grows 8–10' tall.

Lilyturf
Liriope

L. muscari 'Monroe White'

Resistant to drought, heat, humidity and most pests and diseases, lilyturf is one tough plant. Use it in small pots that tend to dry out quickly because not much else will survive in tiny pots.

Growing
Lilyturf grows best in **light shade** or **partial shade** but tolerates both full sun and full shade well. The potting mix should be **humus rich, acidic, moist** and **well drained**. Fertilize monthly during the growing season with quarter-strength fertilizer. Where they are not hardy, plants will have to be stored in a shed or garage in winter or treated like annuals and replaced in spring.

Tips
Lilyturf is a good choice as a container groundcover in warm coastal gardens. If you have containers of shrubs and trees that you don't want to replant with annuals every year, lilyturf will form a low, dense mat of narrow, arching foliage with spikes of blue, purple or white flowers. It also makes an attractive addition to a mixed container.

Recommended
L. muscari forms low clumps of strap-like, evergreen leaves. It bears spikes of purple flowers from late summer on. **'Big Blue'** bears large spikes of purple-blue flowers. **'Monroe White'** has white flowers. **'Pee Dee Gold Ingot'** has golden yellow to chartreuse leaves that mature to bright yellow. It bears light purple flowers. **'Variegata'** has green-and-white-striped leaves and purple flowers.

Features: clump-forming, evergreen perennial; narrow, grass-like, dark green -foliage; spikes of blue, purple or white, fall flowers **Height:** 8–18" **Spread:** 18" **Hardiness:** zones 6–10

Lobelia

Lobelia

L. *erinus* cultivars and others (above)
L. *erinus* (below)

Features: bushy to upright habit; purple, blue, pink, white or red, summer to fall flowers **Height:** 4–24" **Spread:** 6" or more **Hardiness:** zones 4–8; annual

Both the annual and perennial selections of lobelia are interesting to use in container gardens. Each adds a unique touch.

Growing

All lobelias grow well in **full sun** or **partial shade**, with partial shade preferable for annual lobelia in hot and humid areas. The potting mix should be **humus rich, moist** and **well drained**. Fertilize every two to four weeks during the growing season with quarter-strength fertilizer. Cardinal flower tolerates wet soil. Cardinal flower should be moved to a sheltered location, preferably an unheated garage, in winter.

Tips

Use annual lobelia in mixed containers or hanging baskets. The delicate, airy appearance adds a glaze of color that looks particularly attractive with broad-leaved plants such as hosta and lady's mantle.

Cardinal flower has a more upright habit, and its often bronzy foliage gives mixed containers an elegant appearance. Its ability to grow in moist to wet soil makes it suitable for boggy containers with other moisture lovers.

Recommended

L. cardinalis (cardinal flower) is a perennial that forms an upright clump of bronzy green foliage. It bears spikes of bright red flowers in summer and fall.

L. erinus (annual lobelia) may be rounded and bushy or low and trailing. It bears flowers in shades of blue, purple, red, pink or white. **Laguna Series** has heat-resistant, trailing plants with flowers in a variety of colors. **Riviera Series** has flowers in shades of blue and purple on compact, bushy plants.

L. x speciosa (hybrid cardinal flower) is a vigorous, bushy perennial. Hardiness varies from hybrid to hybrid. It bears flowers in shades of red, blue, purple, pink or white in summer and fall.

Trim annual lobelia back after the first wave of flowers. It will stop blooming in the hottest part of summer but usually revives in fall.

L. erinus 'Sapphire' with lamium and impatiens (above)
L. cardinalis (below)

Lotus Vine
Lotus

L. berthelotii with pansies

Lotus vine is also known as parrot's beak, coral gem and pelican's beak, names that make reference to the flowers' appearance.

Features: bushy or trailing habit; orange, red or yellow, summer through fall flowers
Height: 6–8" **Spread:** 36" or more **Hardiness:** tender perennial grown as an annual

*D*on't plant lotus vine solely for the flowers; this annual is highly sought after for its unique, ferny foliage and bushy but trailing growth habit.

Growing

Lotus vine grows well in **full sun** or **partial shade**. The potting mix should be **well drained**. This annual tolerates hot and dry locations. Pinch the new tips back in late spring or early summer to promote bushier growth. Fertilize monthly with quarter-strength fertilizer.

Tips

Lotus vine is most effective when its striking, unique foliage is allowed to cascade over the side of a decorative pot, window box or planter. The flowers are bright and colorful, and they contrast with the silvery green, ferny foliage. Lotus vine complements purple- and yellow-flowering annuals and chartreuse- or bronze-leaved foliage plants very nicely.

Recommended

L. x **'Amazon Sunset'** is a Proven Winners hybrid with gray-green, needle-like foliage and vibrantly hued yellow-orange flowers that darken toward the edge. Although most lotus vines need night temperatures of 40° F to bloom, this one will flower with temperatures up to 55° F.

L. berthelotii is a trailing plant with silvery stems covered in fine, soft, needle-like foliage. Small clusters of vivid orange to scarlet flowers that resemble lobster claws are borne in spring and summer.

L. hirsutus is a bushy or trailing perennial with fine, gray-green foliage. It bears pink-flushed, white flowers in summer and fall.

Lungwort
Pulmonaria

P. GAELIC SUNSET with impatiens and wishbone flower

The wide array of lungworts have highly attractive foliage that ranges in color from apple green to silver-spotted and olive to dark emerald green.

Growing

Lungworts prefer **partial to full shade**. The potting mix should be **humus rich, moist** and **well drained**. Mix in compost or earthworm castings. Fertilize monthly during the growing season with half-strength fertilizer. Deadhead to keep plants tidy by removing the flower stems after flowering is finished. Cut the leaves right to the ground if they show signs of mildew or otherwise look ugly. Fresh, attractive growth will appear. In colder areas, move plants to a sheltered location in winter.

Tips

Lungworts are useful, attractive plants for shady and woodland-themed containers.

Their interesting foliage complements and contrasts brightly colored flowers.

Recommended

P. longifolia (long-leaved lungwort) forms a dense clump of long, narrow, white-spotted, green leaves and bears clusters of blue flowers. Cultivars are available.

P. officinalis (common lungwort) forms a loose clump of white-spotted, evergreen foliage. The flowers open pink and mature to blue. Cultivars are available.

P. saccharata (Bethlehem sage) forms a compact clump of large, white-spotted, evergreen leaves and purple, red or white flowers. Many cultivars and hybrids with other lungwort species are available.

Features: clump-forming perennial; decorative, mottled foliage; blue, red, pink or white, spring flowers **Height:** 8–24" **Spread:** 8–24" **Hardiness:** zones 3–8

Lysimachia
Lysimachia

L. nummularia with blue fescue, snapdragon, fan flower and lamium

Not to be confused with purple loosestrife (Lythrum salicaria), which has been banned because of its invasive nature in wetlands, true loosestrife works well just about anywhere in the garden.

Also called: loosestrife **Features:** yellow or white flowers in spring and summer **Height:** 2–36" **Spread:** 18–36" **Hardiness:** zones 2–8

These vigorous, carefree plants will enjoy a spot in a moist bog-themed container planting.

Growing
Lysimachia grows well in **full sun** or **partial shade**. The potting mix should be **moist** and **well drained**, though this plant tolerates wet soil. Fertilize monthly during the growing season with quarter- to half-strength fertilizer. In colder areas, move containers to a sheltered location protected from temperature fluctuations in winter.

Tips
The low, spreading creeping Jenny will form a dense mat that spills over the edges of your containers and creeps into any others you have positioned close by. The contrasting foliage of golden creeping Jenny works well planted with lungwort or blue-leaved hosta. Gooseneck loosestrife is a good upright companion plant for a mixed container.

Recommended
L. clethroides (gooseneck loosestrife) is a bushy, upright plant with deep green foliage that turns brilliant bronzy red in fall. Tall spikes of white flowers, bent like a goose's neck, are borne on purple stems in mid- and late summer.

L. nummularia (creeping Jenny) is a prostrate, spreading plant with trailing stems. It bears bright yellow flowers on and off all summer. **'Goldilocks'** (golden creeping Jenny) produces golden foliage with yellow flowers.

Maidenhair Fern
Adiantum

These charming, delicate-looking ferns add a graceful touch to any shady container planting. Their unique habit and texture will stand out in any combination.

Growing

Maidenhair fern grows well in **light to partial shade** but tolerates full shade. The potting mix should be **humus rich, slightly acidic** and **moist**. Fertilize monthly during the growing season with quarter-strength fertilizer.

Maidenhair fern is frost tender. Move northern maidenhair fern to a sheltered location in winter. Bring giant maidenhair fern indoors and keep it in a cool, bright room in winter. Like other ferns, this one likes high humidity. Fill a tray with pebbles and water and place it beneath the plant in dry areas.

Tips

These lovely ferns will do well in any shaded spot. Include them in mixed containers, where they make beautiful, arching companions to other shade-lovers such as hosta, lungwort and coral bells. They also look nice with colorful flowers.

Recommended

A. formosum (giant maidenhair fern) is a tender species that is sometimes grown as a houseplant. It has stunning, arching fronds that give the whole plant a cascading appearance. It is worth searching for and including in a mixed container, where it is sure to be an elegant beauty.

A. pedatum (northern maidenhair fern) is a hardy perennial that forms a spreading mound of delicate, arching fronds arranged in a horseshoe or circular pattern. Its light green leaflets stand out against the black stems and turn bright

A. pedatum with dracaena, oxalis and coleus

yellow in fall. These ferns look especially attractive in shiny, black ceramic or painted metal pots. The pot will color echo the dark stems.

Features: deciduous fern; summer and fall foliage; habit **Height:** 12–36" **Spread:** 12–24" **Hardiness:** zones 3–8; tender perennial grown as an annual

Mandevilla
Mandevilla

M. splendens cultivar

With their showy, trumpet-shaped flowers, these easy-care vines set a tropical tone.

Growing

Mandevilla grows in **full sun** in coastal areas and **partial shade** inland. The potting mix should be **well drained**. To avoid root rot, plant mandevilla slightly higher than the surrounding soil. Do not allow mandevilla to sit in cold, wet mix. Water when the top inch of your planting medium feels dry. Fertilize monthly with an all-purpose fertilizer. Pinch for bushiness; flowers bloom on new wood. In cold areas, move these frost-tender plants inside near a sunny window and keep them on the dry side.

Tips

Mandevillas can be trained to climb almost any sturdy structure. They look wonderful as specimens in trellised containers and are stunning in hanging baskets.

Recommended

M. x *amabilis* **'Alice du Pont'** is a summer-flowering, pink climber with a red center that can reach 15–20' tall. It prefers partial shade and looks beautiful on a trellis. **'Tango Twirl'** from Monrovia has unusual soft pink, double flowers with green, glossy leaves.

M. splendens **'Red Fury'** has bright red flowers with golden throats on flowers that bloom year-round in mild climates. Vining stems grow to 6' long.

M. x **'Sunmandecrim'** (Sun Parasol Series) from Suntory includes plants flowering in white, red, pink or crimson.

Features: evergreen vine; can also be trimmed as a bush; trumpet-shaped flowers **Height:** 5–20' in containers **Spread:** 2–5' if grown vertically **Hardiness:** zones 10–11; tender perennial

Maple
Acer

A. *ginnala* 'Bailey Compact'

Maples are attractive all year long, boasting delicate flowers in spring, attractive foliage and hanging samaras in summer, vibrant leaf color in fall and interesting bark and branch structures in winter.

Growing
Maples do well in **full sun** or **light shade**. The potting mix should be **humus rich** and **well drained**. Fertilize no more than monthly during the

Maple fruits, called samaras, have wings that act like miniature helicopter rotors and help in seed dispersal.

Features: small, multi-stemmed, deciduous tree or large shrub; colorful or decorative foliage that turns stunning shades of red, yellow or orange in fall **Height:** 2–15' **Spread:** 2–15' **Hardiness:** zones 2–8

A. palmatum 'Bloodgood' (above)

A. japonicum (center), A. griseum (below)

growing season with quarter-strength fertilizer. Tender maples should be moved into a shed or garage in winter. Hardy maples will do fine in a spot protected from temperature fluctuations.

Tips

Maples can be used as specimen trees in containers on patios or terraces. A Japanese-style garden can be created in containers with a maple or two to add height and volume. Almost all maples can be used to create bonsai specimens.

Recommended

A. ginnala (amur maple) is an extremely hardy, rounded to spreading tree that has attractive, dark green leaves, bright red samaras and smooth bark with distinctive vertical striping. The fall foliage is often a brilliant crimson. The color develops best in full sun, but the tree will also grow well in light shade.

A. griseum (paperbark maple) is a rounded to oval tree with exfoliating, orange-brown bark that peels and curls away from the trunk in papery strips. The foliage turns red, orange or yellow in fall. (Zones 4–8)

A. japonicum (fullmoon maple, Japanese maple) is an open, spreading tree or large shrub. The leaves turn stunning shades of yellow, orange or red in fall. (Zones 5–7)

A. palmatum (Japanese maple) is a rounded, spreading or cascading, small tree that develops red, yellow or orange fall color. Two distinct groups of cultivars have been developed. Types without dissected leaves, derived from *A. p.* var. *atropurpureum*, are grown for their purple foliage. Types with dissected leaves, derived from *A. p.* var. *dissectum*, have foliage so deeply lobed and divided that it appears fern-like or even thread-like. The leaves can be green, red or purple. (Zones 6–8)

Million Bells
Calibrachoa

Million bells are charming plants that will bloom continuously throughout the growing season. They look like cascading petunias and were once classified as such. Recent discoveries of chromosomal and breeding differences prompted reclassification to a different genus.

Growing
Million bells prefer **full sun**. The potting mix should be **moist** and **well drained**. Fertilize every two weeks with half-strength fertilizer. Although they prefer to be watered regularly, million bells are fairly drought resistant in cool and warm climates. Million bells do not need deadheading but will bounce back after a light mid-season shearing. The flowers will bloom well into fall. Hardy to about 23° F, these plants are frost-tender and can be treated as perennials in mild-winter areas.

Tips
Million bells are deservedly popular for planters and hanging baskets. They can stand alone, filling and trailing over the edge of just about any container, and also make lovely additions to mixed containers, where the colorful flowers will stand out against a background of any shade of green, bronze or chartreuse. Try it with everything from bidens, nemesia and verbena to salvia and grasses.

Recommended
C. **hybrids** have a dense, trailing habit. They all bear small, yellow-centered flowers that resemble petunias. There are many cultivars available, and more beautiful plants with a wider range of flower colors become available each year. Two main series for these plants

C. Superbells Series 'Trailing Blue'

are **Million Bells Series** and **Superbells Series**. Both offer plants with flowers in shades of blue, pink, red, yellow, orange or white. Several bicolored options are also available, including yellow/orange, mottled and pink-veined/white.

Also called: calibrachoa **Features:** trailing habit; pink, purple, blue, red, yellow, orange, white or bicolored flowers **Height:** 6–12" **Spread:** 24" **Hardiness:** tender perennial grown as an annual

Mondo Grass
Ophiopogon

O. planiscapus NIGRA

This plant is not a grass at all—it is a member of the lily family.

Features: low, clump-forming habit; uniquely colored foliage; lavender, pink or white flowers **Height:** 4–12" **Spread:** 6–12" **Hardiness:** zones 5–9; perennial grown as an annual

Mondo grass is an excellent accent and contrast plant. The foliage makes a stunning background to highlight any brightly colored plant or flower.

Growing
Mondo grass grows best in **full sun to light shade**. The potting mix should be **humus rich, moist** and **well drained**. Fertilize monthly during the growing season with quarter- to half-strength fertilizer. In colder areas, treat these plants like annuals or move containers to an unheated garage or shed in winter to protect them from temperature fluctuations.

Tips
Use this short, grassy perennial in front of other grasses and accent it with a collection of river stones or glass pebbles. It will have a calming effect when used by itself in a pot. The foliage contrasts nicely with many colorful plants.

Recommended
O. japonicus (mondo grass, monkey grass) produces an evergreen mat of lush, dark green, grass-like foliage. Short spikes of white, occasionally lilac-tinged flowers emerge in summer, followed by metallic blue fruit. Many cultivars are available. Plants are hardy to zone 6 with protection.

O. planiscapus 'Ebknizam' ('Ebony Night') has curving, almost black leaves and dark lavender flowers. NIGRA (black mondo grass, black lilyturf), a Proven Selection by Proven Winners, is a clumping, spreading plant with dark purple, almost black leaves and pink to mauve flowers.

Monkey Flower

Mimulus

The name alone makes these good plants for a tropical-themed container garden. A wide range of colors and a floriferous habit are bonuses.

Growing

Monkey flowers prefer **light shade** or **partial shade** with protection from the afternoon sun. The potting mix should be **humus rich** and **moist to wet**. Mix in compost or earthworm castings. Fertilize every two weeks in summer with quarter- to half-strength fertilizer. In areas that receive frost, plants can be brought indoors at the end of summer and grown as houseplants in a cool, bright room until spring.

Tips

Monkey flowers are excellent in a bog-themed mixed container because they naturally grow alongside streams. Many of the other moisture-loving plants are foliage plants or flower for only a short time, so these colorful bloomers are a welcome addition.

Recommended

M. aurantiacus is an upright to relaxed plant with glossy, sticky, bright green leaves. It bears dark red, orange or yellow flowers in late summer.

M. x hybridus is a group of upright plants with spotted flowers. **'Calypso Mixed'** has flowers in a wide range of colors. **Mystic Series** are compact, early-flowering plants that offer a wide range of bright flower colors in solids or bicolors.

M. luteus (yellow monkey flower) has a spreading habit and attractive yellow flowers sometimes spotted with red or purple.

M. x hybridus 'Mystic'

The markings on the face of the flowers look like monkey faces to some people.

Features: bushy, upright or trailing habit; flowers in bright and pastel shades of orange, yellow, burgundy, pink, red, cream or bicolors **Height:** 6–12" **Spread:** 12–24" **Hardiness:** zones 6–9; semi-hardy perennial grown as an annual

Nasturtium

Tropaeolum

T. majus 'Alaska' with sweet potato vine and others

There is almost nothing as lovely as the wonderful red, orange or yellow flowers dotting a planting of nasturtiums as they tumble over the edge of a tall terracotta pot.

Growing

Nasturtiums prefer **full sun** but tolerate some shade. The potting mix should be **light, moist** and **well drained**. Too much fertilizer will result in lots of leaves and very few flowers, so fertilize no more than monthly with quarter-strength fertilizer. Let the soil drain completely between waterings.

Features: trailing, climbing or bushy habit; bright red, orange, yellow, scarlet, pink, cream, gold, white or bicolored flowers; attractive round, sometimes variegated foliage; edible leaves and flowers **Height:** 12–18" for dwarf varieties; up to 10' for trailing varieties **Spread:** equal to height **Hardiness:** annual

Tips

Nasturtiums are used in containers and hanging baskets. The climbing varieties can be grown up trellises or left to spill over the edge of a container and ramble around. The bushy selections can be used in mixed containers with other red-, yellow- or orange-flowered plants, or with other edible-flowered plants such as pansies for a themed container.

Recommended

T. majus is a bushy plant or a trailing or climbing plant. It bears bright red, yellow or orange flowers all summer. The bright green leaves are round with wavy margins. **'Alaska'** has cream-mottled foliage and a bushy habit. **'Jewel'** has bushy plants with flowers in shades of red, scarlet, pink, yellow, cream or orange, some with darker-veined throats.

Nemesia
Nemesia

N. SUNSATIA PINEAPPLE and others

Nemesias make a bright and colorful addition to the front of a mixed container planting.

Growing
Nemesias grow best in **full sun**. The potting mix should be **slightly acidic, moist** and **well drained**. Regular watering will keep these plants blooming through summer. Fertilize every two weeks with quarter-strength fertilizer when plants are actively growing and blooming. Nemesias benefit from being cut back hard when the flowering cycle slows down.

Tips
Nemesias are beautiful little plants that are best used in mixed containers because they tend to stop blooming during the hottest part of summer. Many nemesia varieties are fragrant and attract butterflies.

Recommended
N. **hybrids** are bushy and mound forming or trailing and have bright green foliage. They bear flowers in shades of blue, purple, white, pink, red or yellow, often in bicolors. **'Bluebird'** bears lavender blue flowers on low, bushy plants. **Carnival Series** plants are compact and bear many flowers in yellow, white, orange, pink or red. Look for even brighter colors in Proven Winners' new **'Juicy Fruits'** line. **'KLM'** has bicolored blue and white flowers with yellow throats. Proven Winners Selection SUNSATIA SERIES includes colorful cultivars that may be bushy or trailing and several that are heat resistant.

Features: bushy, mound-forming habit; red, blue, purple, pink, white, yellow, orange or bicolored flowers **Height:** 6–24" **Spread:** 4–12" **Hardiness:** tender perennial grown as an annual

Nicotiana
Nicotiana

N. alata Nicki Series and *N. sylvestris* with cleome

These bushy, sticky plants topped with clusters of tubular flowers attract night-flying pollinators such as moths. Plant the scented variety in a garden where its fragrance can waft through windows at night.

Growing
Nicotiana will grow equally well in **full sun, light shade** or **partial shade**. The potting mix should be **humus rich, moist** and **well drained**. Fertilize every two weeks with half-strength fertilizer. Deadhead to promote bloom.

Tips
The dwarf selections seem best suited for small mixed containers, but the taller selections make excellent center plants with low, bushy and trailing plants surrounding their feet.

Recommended
N. alata is an upright plant that has a strong, sweet fragrance. **Merlin Series** has dwarf plants with red, pink, purple, white or pale green flowers. **Nicki Series** has compact or dwarf plants with fragrant blooms in many colors.

N. **'Lime Green'** is an upright plant that bears clusters of lime green flowers.

N. sylvestris is a tall, upright plant that bears white blooms that are fragrant in the evening.

Nicotiana was originally cultivated for the wonderful scent of its flowers. At first, the flowers were only green and opened only in the evening and at night. In attempts to expand the variety of colors and have the flowers open during the day, the popular scent has, in some cases, been lost. All parts of the plant are poisonous.

Also called: flowering tobacco **Features:** sticky, rosette-forming to bushy, upright habit; red, pink, green, yellow, white or purple, sometimes fragrant flowers **Height:** 1–5' **Spread:** 12" **Hardiness:** annual

Oregano
Origanum

Oregano is a lovely, fragrant plant with a compact, rounded habit and decorative foliage.

Growing
Oregano grows best in **full sun**. The potting mix should be **neutral to alkaline** and **well drained**. Fertilize no more than once a month during the growing season with quarter-strength fertilizer. In winter, move hardy plants to a sheltered location; where they are not hardy, move them to an unheated shed or garage.

Tips
Try growing several different oreganos in individual containers of different heights to create a grouping, or plant different herbs in each pot for a more varied display. Pinch off the leaves to use in spaghetti sauce or other dishes.

Recommended
O. laevigatum is a shrubby, upright perennial that bears rosy purple flowers. **'Hopley's Purple'** bears dark purple flowers and is hardy to zone 6.

O. roundifolium **'Kent Beauty'** is a showy spiller with pink summer flowers and gray-green leaves. (Zones 7–10)

O. vulgare subsp. *hirtum* (oregano, Greek oregano) is a low-growing, bushy plant with hairy, gray-green leaves and white flowers. **'Aureum'** has bright golden leaves and pink flowers. **'Aureum Crispum'** has a spreading habit and curly, golden leaves. **'Zorba Red'** has a spreading habit with bright red-purple bracts and white flowers. **'Zorba White'** has greenish bracts and white flowers.

O. vulgare var. *hirtum* 'Aureum' with marigold, parsley and tarragon

Features: bushy perennial; fragrant, sometimes colorful foliage; white or pink, summer flowers **Height:** 10–24" **Spread:** 8–12" **Hardiness:** zones 5–10

Oxalis
Oxalis

O. vulcanicola 'Zinfandel' and others

Tiny, decorative pots of O. crassipes *are often found in garden centers and gift shops around St. Patrick's Day.*

Features: bushy or spreading habit; colorful foliage; yellow, white or pink flowers **Height:** 6–12" **Spread:** 6–12" or more **Hardiness:** tender perennial grown as an annual

Oxalis readily fills little spaces with dense, lustrous foliage and teeny, tiny flowers that never cease to amaze.

Growing
Oxalis prefers **full sun** or **partial shade** but tolerates full shade with reduced flowering. The potting mix should be **humus rich** and **well drained**. Fertilize every two weeks with quarter-strength fertilizer.

Tips
Oxalis is becoming increasingly popular for container culture, with new varieties appearing annually. Oxalis is stunning by itself and also works well mixed with other plants such as bacopa, African daisy, million bells and verbena.

Recommended
O. crassipes is a vigorous, mound-forming species with bright green leaves and lemon yellow flowers. **'Alba'** bears green leaves and tiny, white flowers. It is tolerant of extreme heat and drought. **'Rosea'** has pink flowers.

O. regnellii is a vigorous, shade-loving species. It produces large, shamrock-shaped foliage and dainty flowers. Watch for the CHARMED SERIES from Proven Winners.

O. vulcanicola is a small, bushy, spreading plant with reddish stems, green foliage flushed with red, and yellow flowers with purple-red veining. **'Copper Tones'** and **'Molten Lava'** have gold foliage with a touch of rust and buttery yellow flowers at the tips of reddish stems. **'Zinfandel,'** a Proven Selection by Proven Winners, produces dark burgundy, almost black foliage and tiny, vivid yellow blooms.

Pansy
Viola

V. x *wittrockiana* cultivar with vinca, coral bells and dracaena

Colorful and cheerful, pansy flowers are a welcome sight in spring after a long, dreary winter.

Growing
Pansies prefer **full sun** but tolerate partial shade. The potting mix should be **moist** and **well drained**. Fertilize every two weeks during the growing season with quarter-strength fertilizer. Pansies do best when the weather is cool and often die back completely in summer. Plants may rejuvenate in fall, but it is

Johnny-jump-ups self-seed prolifically and may turn up from year to year in their original container and others, too.

Features: blue, purple, red, orange, yellow, pink or white, bicolored or multi-colored flowers **Height:** 3–10" **Spread:** 6–12" **Hardiness:** zones 5–9; often grown as an annual

V. x *wittrockiana* cultivar with calla lily (above)
V. x *wittrockiana* (below)

often easier to plant new ones. Dead-head to keep these plants blooming and to prevent self-seeding.

Tips

Pansies make good companions for spring-flowering bulbs and primroses. A pot of spring pansies set where you can see it from indoors will remind you that summer is just around the corner. For a dramatic spring display, use pansies around the base of potted tulips and daffodils.

Recommended

V. cornuta (horned violet, viola) is a low-growing, spreading plant. The flowers are usually in shades of blue, purple or white. **Chalon Hybrids** bear ruffled, bicolored or multi-colored flowers in shades of blue, red, rose or white. **Sorbet Series** has a wide color range. Planted in fall, they flower until the ground freezes and may surprise you with another show in spring. '**Sorbet Yesterday, Today and Tomorrow**' bears flowers that open white and gradually turn purple as they mature.

V. tricolor (Johnny-jump-up) is a popular species. The flowers are purple, white and yellow, usually in combination, though several varieties have flowers in a single color, often purple.

V. x *wittrockiana* (pansy) comes in blue, purple, red, orange, yellow, pink or white, often multi-colored or with face-like markings. '**Antique Shades Mix**' offers pastel combinations of plum, yellow, apricot, rust and cream. '**Can Can Mix**' bears frilly flowers with ruffled edges in bicolored and multi-colored combinations of yellow, purple, red, white, pink and blue. **Imperial Series** includes plants that bear large flowers in a range of unique colors. '**Imperial Frosty Rose**' has flowers with deep rose pink centers that gradually pale to white near the edges of the petals.

Parsley
Petroselinum

The bright green color of parsley provides an unmatched display to fill in the spaces among the other plants in your containers.

Growing
Parsley grows well in **full sun** or **partial shade**. The potting mix should be **humus rich, moist** and **well drained**. Fertilize every two weeks with quarter-strength fertilizer. Direct sow seeds because the plants resent transplanting. The seeds can take several weeks to sprout. Soak the seeds in warm water for 24 hours before sowing to speed up germination.

Tips
Containers of parsley can be kept close to the house for easy picking if you are growing it for eating or garnish—you could have several pots containing different herbs. Parsley is also a fantastic mixer plant for containers. Its bushy growth fills in quickly, and the bright green creates a good background for bright red, scarlet or orange flowers in particular.

Recommended
P. crispum forms a clump of bright green, divided leaves. This plant is a biennial but is usually grown as an annual because it is the leaves that are desired, not the flowers or seeds. Cultivars may have flat or curly leaves. Flat leaves are more flavorful and curly are more decorative. Dwarf cultivars are also available.

P. crispum with others

Parsley leaves make a tasty and nutritious addition to salads. Tear freshly picked leaves and sprinkle them over your mixed greens.

Features: clump-forming habit; attractive foliage **Height:** 8–24" **Spread:** 12–24" **Hardiness:** zones 5–8; biennial grown as an annual

Penstemon
Penstemon

P. LILLIPUT ROSE, a Proven Winners Selection, with nemesia and coleus

Recent interest in drought-tolerant gardening has ignited attention to these attractive plants.

Growing
Penstemons prefer **full sun** but tolerate partial shade. The potting mix should be **very well drained**. Add one-third sand or perlite to the potting mix to ensure quick drainage. These plants are quite drought tolerant. Fertilize once at the beginning of the growing season at half the normal rate with slow-release fertilizer. Move containers to a sheltered location protected from temperature fluctuations in winter.

Tips
These plants tend to be tall and slender and are prone to falling over unless surrounded by supportive neighbors. They are ideal for mixed containers.

Recommended
P. barbatus (beardlip penstemon) is an upright, rounded perennial. Red or pink flowers are borne from early summer to early fall. **'Hyacinth Mix'** is a mix of pink, lilac, blue and scarlet.

P. digitalis **'Husker Red'** is an upright semi-evergreen that has red stems and red-purple new foliage. It bears white flowers veined with red all summer.

P. fruticosus **'Purple Haze'** is a mound-forming, evergreen subshrub. It bears purple flowers prolifically in late spring. When placed near a wall edge or overhang, it will trail over the side.

P. gentianoides **'Hartweg'** has showy blooms in white, pink, red and purple on the same plant and grows 24–36" tall and wide.

Also called: beard-tongue **Features:** white, yellow, pink, purple or red, spring, summer or fall flowers **Height:** 18"–5' **Spread:** 12–36" **Hardiness:** zones 4–9

Perilla

Perilla

Perilla is well known for its tolerance of summer heat and will easily compete with some of the most aggressive summer annuals. Recently, breeders have introduced more decorative selections to the market, making perilla highly sought after.

Growing

Perilla prefers **full sun** or **partial shade**. The potting mix should be **fertile, moist** and **well drained**. Potting mix amended with compost or well-composted manure is of added benefit. Plants can be pinched for more bushiness. Perilla may self-seed prolifically.

Tips

Perilla is the perfect alternative to coleus and is an ideal complement to brightly colored annuals and perennials in decorative containers. Use a deep bronze perilla in the center of a terracotta pot and surround it with bright orange and yellow marigolds for a strong combination that can handle the heat.

Recommended

P. frutescens is a vigorous annual with deeply toothed, medium green, purple-flecked, cinnamon-lemon–flavored leaves. Tiny, white flowers are borne on spikes in summer, but this annual is grown more for its ornate, colorful foliage. **'Atropurpurea'** (beefsteak plant)

P. 'Magellanica,' a Proven Selections plant from Proven Winners, and others

bears dark purple-red leaves. **Var. *crispa*** (var. *nankinensis*; 'Crispa') has dark bronze to purple foliage with very frilly leaf margins. **'Magilla'** ('Magilla Purple') bears multi-colored leaves of purple, green, white and pink, and **'Magilla Vanilla'** bears white and green leaves.

Also called: shiso, Chinese basil **Features:** bushy, vigorous habit; ornate, colorful foliage **Height:** 12–24" **Spread:** 12–24" **Hardiness:** annual

Petunia
Petunia

P. x *hybrida* with English ivy and reed palm

Petunias can be enjoyed as cut flowers. Regular cutting of blooms helps keep the plants bushy. The purple and white petunias tend to be the most fragrant.

Features: bushy to trailing habit; summer flowers in shades of pink, blue, purple, red, coral, yellow or white, or bicolored **Height:** 6–18" **Spread:** 12–24" or wider **Hardiness:** annual

For speedy growth, prolific blooming, ease of care and a huge number of varieties, petunias are hard to beat. The rekindling of interest in petunias resulted largely from the development of many exciting new varieties.

Growing

Petunias prefer **full sun**. The potting mix should be **well drained**. Fertilize no more than monthly with quarter-strength fertilizer. Pinch halfway back in midsummer to keep plants bushy and to encourage new growth and flowers.

Tips

Use petunias in containers and hanging baskets. Planted alone, their bushy growth will fill a container and spill over the edge. The rich colors of their flowers also make them excellent companions for other annuals as well as for any container plantings of shrubs or small trees.

Recommended

P. x *hybrida* is a large group of popular, sun-loving annuals that fall into three categories: grandifloras, with the largest flowers; multifloras, bearing many medium-sized flowers; and millifloras, with the smallest flowers.

P. **Storm Series** are grandiflora petunias that are weather and disease tolerant and bear large blooms in a range of colors.

P. **Supertunia Series** offers single and double flowers in a wide range of pinks and purples, but there are also red, white and yellow selections. Look for the mini series that forms a long trail of blossoms from top to bottom.

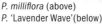
P. milliflora (above)
P. 'Lavender Wave'(below)

P. **Wave Series** are vigorous, low-growing, spreading plants that bloom almost non-stop in a range of colors. They are tolerant of rain and cold. Look for **'Blue,' 'Lavender,' 'Misty Lilac,' 'Pink,' 'Purple'** and **'Rose.' Tidal Wave Series** are upright, spreading plants. Selections include **'Cherry,' 'Pink Hot,' 'Purple'** and **'Silver.' Easy Wave Series** are mound-forming petunias similar to the original Wave Series, but a little taller. Easy Wave selections include **'Blue,' 'Coral Reef,' 'Mystic Pink,' 'Pink,' 'Red,' 'Rosy Dawn,' 'Salmon,' 'Shell Pink'** and **'White.'**

Phlox
Phlox

P. 'Intensia Lilac Rose' with pentunia, sweet flag and lamium

Phlox makes excellent cut flowers and also attracts hummingbirds. New hybrids are less prone to powdery mildew and are more resistant to heat and humidity.

Growing
Phlox does best in **full sun** with good air movement to lessen opportunities for powdery mildew. The potting mix should be **moist** and **well drained**. Phlox likes cool summer temperatures and low humidity.

Cut back the top third after the first bloom to get more flowers. Avoid crowding to avoid mildew.

Tips
Phlox looks good in mixed containers with million bells, cuphea, nemesia, euphorbia, bidens and others.

Recommended
P. drummondii hybrids in the **Intensia Series** from Proven Winners is a large-flowered variety that is fragrant and resistant to heat, humidity and mildew. Colors are in the pink and white range with standouts '**Cabernet**,' a beautiful purple red, and '**Star Brite**,' white with intense purple-pink through each petal.

P. paniculata **Volcano™ Phlox** from Tesselaar Plants is fragrant and disease resistant and grows 24–30" tall. It is available in purple, red, ruby, white and two bicolors: pink with red eye and pink with white eye. The flowers bloom June through September.

Features: mounding or trailing habit; white, pink or purple flowers, some bicolored
Height: 10–30" **Spread:** 10–12" **Hardiness:** zones 9–10; grown as an annual

Phormium

Phormium

*D*ramatic, drought-tolerant plants with sword-like leaves, phormiums make a strong statement in large pots.

Growing

Phormiums grow best in **full sun** but appreciate some protection from the hot afternoon sun. The potting mix should be **moist** and **well drained**. Fertilize every two weeks during the growing season with half-strength fertilizer. Once established, these hardy plants can take a variety of exposures and moisture levels. In cold areas, plants grown in containers can be overwintered in a bright, cool, frost-free location indoors.

Tips

Use phormiums in container plantings near entryways and walkways. Their bold and exotic foliage will draw the eye and encourage visitors to come closer.

Recommended

P. '**Sundowner**' forms a clump of broad, upright foliage. The light, bronzy green foliage is margined with pink and yellow. This variety will not overwinter outdoors.

P. tenax (New Zealand flax) forms a large clump of long, stiff, dark green leaves with gray-green undersides. '**Aurora**' has bronzy green leaves striped with pink, yellow and red. '**Limelight**' offers lime green leaves and bronze flowers. '**Maori Maiden**' has arching, pink- to rose-colored leaves with green margins; protect it from hot afternoon sun. '**Tiny Tiger**' has gray-green leaves edged with cream and grows only 24" tall and 36" wide. '**Veitchianum**' has cream-striped, green leaves.

P. '**Yellow Wave**' forms a clump of yellow-green leaves striped with darker green.

P. tenax cultivar with echeveria and hens and chicks

Large, loose, spikes of small flowers are sometimes produced in summer.

Also called: New Zealand flax **Features:** clump-forming habit; green, black, red or yellow, often multi-colored and striped foliage **Height:** 2–8' **Spread:** 2–8' **Hardiness:** zones 9–10; tender perennial grown as an annual

Piggyback Plant
Tolmiea

T. menziesii

Piggyback plant uniquely produces new plantlets from the surface of an existing leaf, hence the common name.

Growing

Piggyback plant grows best in **full shade, light shade** or **partial shade** with protection from the hot afternoon sun. The potting mix should be **moist** and **well drained**. Fertilize monthly during the growing season with quarter-strength fertilizer. Spray the leaves often with a strong jet of water to keep them free of spider mites, which can be a problem during warm weather. Overwinter plants in a cool, bright room where they are not hardy. Where they are hardy, move them to a sheltered location protected from temperature fluctuations. Piggyback plant is best in cool areas with some humidity.

Tips

Piggyback plant is often grown in hanging baskets. The mounded leaves are weighted down by newly produced foliage, creating a cascading appearance. This plant is an ideal addition to an understory-themed container or for a container on a heavily shaded balcony.

Recommended

T. menziesii is a clump-forming plant with hairy, heart-shaped leaves with toothed edges. Small plantlets emerge where the leaf and stem join. Tiny, tubular, greenish, insignificant flowers open along one side of the leaf. **'Taff's Gold'** produces both solid and variegated leaves, and **'Variegata'** has yellow-splashed leaves.

Also called: thousand mothers, youth-on-age **Features:** clump-forming habit; decorative, piggyback foliage **Height:** 12–18" **Spread:** 12–18" **Hardiness:** zones 6–9; perennial grown as an annual

Plectranthus
Plectranthus

These mound-forming plants, with their often aromatic foliage, eventually develop a more trailing habit.

Growing

Plectranthus grows best in **light shade** or **partial shade**. The potting mix should be **moist** and **well drained**. Fertilize every two weeks with quarter- to half-strength fertilizer.

Tips

These plants make fabulous fillers for mixed containers. Place them near a walkway where people will be able to smell the spicy-scented foliage. Pair them with bananas or canna lilies to add a jungle look to large container gardens.

Recommended

P. argentatus is an upright to spreading plant with silvery green, hairy stems and leaves. It bears clusters of small, bluish white flowers near the ends of stems in summer. It can grow in full sun along the coast but does better with morning sun in the hotter areas.

P. ciliatus is a low-growing, trailing plant with burgundy stems and lilac blue flowers. The dark to olive green, toothed foliage has burgundy undersides. **'Vanilla Twist'** has bright green leaves with white, scalloped margins.

P. coleoides **'Variegata'** from Proven Winners is a trailing, spreading plant with creamy white and green leaves and a fragrance reminiscent of oregano and thyme.

P. forsteri is a mounding then trailing plant with light green, slightly hairy leaves and clusters of small, white or pale purple, summer flowers. **'Marginatus'** has cream-edged leaves.

P. ciliatus 'Vanilla Twist,' a Proven Winners Selection, with sedge, purple fountain grass, English ivy and coleus

P. saccatus **'Mona Lavender'** has dark lavender spiked flowers and leaves with purple undersides. It grows 24–30" tall and flowers until frost.

Also called: Swedish ivy **Features:** bushy to trailing habit; decorative foliage **Height:** 8–30" **Spread:** about 36" **Hardiness:** annual; tender perennial grown as an annual

Poor Man's Orchid

Schizanthus

S. *pinnatus* cultivar

These plants have a short flowering season and are a winter-to-spring annual in California. You can replace them with mums halfway through summer.

Features: pink, red, yellow or purple, usually bicolored flowers whose yellow throats are marked with contrasting streaks and blotches **Height:** 6–24" **Spread:** 9–12" **Hardiness:** annual

Poor man's orchids create spectacular hanging baskets, flowing over the edge and blooming happily in a cocktail of flower shapes and forms.

Growing
Poor man's orchid grows best in **full sun to partial shade** but appreciates some relief from the hot afternoon sun. This plant does not tolerate frost or excess heat and also does quite well planted in light shade. The potting mix should be **fertile, moist** and **well drained**.

Tips
Poor man's orchid can be used in hanging baskets and mixed containers. It does best in cool summer climates. This plant combines well with most other annuals.

Recommended
S. 'Angel Wings' is a trailing hybrid bearing flowers ranging from pale pink to lavender to deep violet.

S. *pinnatus* is an erect plant with light green, fern-like leaves. **'Dwarf Bouquet Mixed'** are short, compact plants, growing to 16" tall, and are good container plants. The flowers are shades of red, orange, pink or orange-yellow. **'Royal Pierrot Mixed'** have rich flowers in pink, purple, purple-blue or white. **'Star Parade'** is a compact variety available in several colors. It grows up to 10" tall.

Purple Fountain Grass
Pennisetum

P. setaceum BURGUNDY GIANT with euphorbia, mondo grass, coleus, English ivy and dwarf plumbago

Purple fountain grass has a graceful, soft but also bold form that makes it a stunning companion in a mixed container. It waves gracefully in the breeze and imparts an intriguing sense of motion to the garden.

Choose a sleek metal or shiny contemporary pot for this decorative grass and mulch the soil with shiny, black, flat stones. You'll have a living piece of modern art for your patio or deck.

Growing
Purple fountain grass grows best in **full sun**. The potting mix should be **well drained**. Fertilize monthly during the growing season with quarter-strength

Features: arching or upright habit; decorative foliage; fuzzy, pink, purple or tan, summer and fall flowers **Height:** 1–6' **Spread:** 18"–4' **Hardiness:** zones 5–11; tender perennial grown as an annual

P. setaceum 'Rubrum' (above)
P. glaucum 'Purple Majesty' with others (below)

fertilizer. Where hardy, purple fountain grass should be overwintered in a sheltered location out of the wind and sun and protected from temperature fluctuations. Where not hardy, it can be cut back in fall and stored in a cool location indoors, or treated as an annual.

Tips

Purple fountain grass is an interesting, low-maintenance alternative to dracaena in mixed containers. The colorful foliage can be used to create color-themed containers with perennials and annuals, whether you complement or contrast the colors.

Recommended

P. alopecuriodes forms clumps of long, narrow, bright green, arching leaves. Soft spikes of tan, pink or purple, fuzzy flowers are produced on long, arching stems in summer and fall. **'Hameln'** is a dwarf cultivar hardy to zone 5. **'Little Bunny'** is an even smaller selection that grows only 12" tall. (Zones 6–9)

P. glaucum **'Purple Majesty'** (purple majesty millet, ornamental millet) has a corn-like growth habit, with a strong central stalk and broad, blackish purple, strap-like leaves. The bottlebrush-like flower spikes are also purple, though the tiny flowers may be yellow. (Zones 8–10)

P. setaceum **'Rubrum'** ('Purpureum,' annual fountain grass) is a dense, mound-forming, tender perennial grown as an annual. It has narrow, dark purple foliage and large, showy, rose red flower spikes from midsummer to fall. **'Prince'** and the smaller **'Princess,'** both Proven Selections by Proven Winners, have fade-proof purple foliage and nodding flower spikes that appear as long as the temperature stays above freezing. (Zones 8–11)

Rhododendron · Azalea

Rhododendron (Azalea)

R. Northern Lights hybrid

These beautiful shrubs are deservedly popular in the northern part of the state where filtered shade and humidity provide ideal growing conditions.

Growing

Rhododendrons prefer **partial shade** or **light shade**. Some varieties will tolerate full sun in cooler areas if the container is kept moist. Provide **shelter** from strong winds. The potting mix should be **fertile, humus rich, acidic, moist** and **well drained**. Add one-third of the container volume of peat moss to the potting mix for the acidity and extra water-holding capacity. Feed in spring at full strength as soon as the container mix warms, then quarter- to half-strength fertilizer every four to six weeks until mid-July. Don't overdo it; rhododendrons in pots are susceptible to fertilizer burn.

Mulch to keep the shallow roots cool in summer. Remove dead and damaged growth in mid-spring. Remove flower clusters. Grasp the base of the cluster

Features: mounding to rounded, evergreen or deciduous shrub; late-winter to early-summer flowers; attractive foliage **Height:** 2–12' **Spread:** 2–12' **Hardiness:** zones 3–11

R. PJM hybrid (above), *R.* Karume hybrid (below)

between your thumb and forefinger and twist to remove the entire cluster. Be careful not to damage the new buds that form directly beneath the flowerheads.

Tips

These gorgeous shrubs are best used as specimen plants underplanted with shade-tolerant groundcovers.

Recommended

A. indica 'California Sunset' from Monrovia is evergreen with variegated pink and white, double blossoms and shiny, green foliage. It grows 3–5' tall and 4–6' wide. (Zones 9–11)

R. **Kurume Hybrids** are deciduous, dwarf azaleas that grow 24–36" tall and wide. The spring flowers bloom mostly in shades of red, pink or white, but shades of orange and purple are also available. (Zones 5–8)

R. **Northern Lights Hybrids** are broad, rounded, deciduous azaleas that grow about 5' tall and 4' wide. These cold-hardy hybrids are available with yellow-orange, yellow, light purple, dark pink, light orange-red or white flowers. (Zones 3–7)

R. **PJM Hybrids** are compact, rounded, dwarf, evergreen rhododendrons. They grow 3–6' tall with an equal spread. These hybrids are weevil resistant and have mostly pink or purple flowers. They are wind and cold resistant and survive cold winters better than the more tender rhododendrons. (Zones 4–8)

R. yakushimanum (Yakushima rhodo-dendron) is a dense, mounding, ever-green rhododendron that grows 36" tall and wide. Rose red buds open to reveal white flowers in mid-spring. The under-side of the foliage is soft and fuzzy. (Zones 5–9)

Rose
Rosa

R. 'Knock Out' (above & below)

There are many roses that will thrive in containers, though most will eventually have to be moved to the garden.

Growing

Roses grow best in **full sun** in areas that receive good air circulation to reduce the chance of disease. The potting mix should be **humus rich, slightly acidic, moist** and **well drained**. Water when the soil feels dry an inch below the surface. Fertilize every two weeks during the growing season with half-strength fertilizer. Deadhead lightly to keep plants tidy and to encourage prolific blooming, except 'Hansa' and 'Knock Out,' which develop attractive hips after the flowers are done.

Features: rounded to arching shrub; often-fragrant, midsummer to fall flowers **Height:** 1–4' **Spread:** 1–4' **Hardiness:** zones 3–9

R. 'Hansa' (above), R. 'Cupcake' (below)

Tips

Bushy modern shrub roses, miniature roses and hardy roses such as the rugosas are the best choices for containers. The miniatures make good companions for mixed containers, while the larger, shrubbier roses make good focal points, perhaps with trailing, white-flowered plants such as bacopas planted around them. Consider a fragrant variety for a large pot on your patio.

Recommended

R. 'Cupcake' is a compact, bushy miniature shrub rose with glossy, green foliage. It produces clusters of light to medium pink flowers all summer. It grows 12–18" tall, with an equal spread. (Zones 5–9)

R. 'George Vancouver' is a hardy, mound-forming Explorer rose that maintains a neat, rounded habit. The medium red, double flowers may be borne singly or in clusters of up to six. It grows about 24" tall and wide.

R. 'Hansa' is a hardy, arching rugosa rose with deeply veined, glossy, leathery foliage. The fragrant, mauve-purple to mauve-red, double flowers are followed by scarlet hips. It grows about 4' tall and wide.

R. 'Knock Out' has an attractive, rounded form with glossy, green leaves that turn to shades of burgundy in fall. The bright cherry red flowers are borne in clusters almost all summer and fall. Orange-red hips last well into winter. It grows about 4' tall and wide and is disease resistant. (Zones 4–9)

Rosemary
Rosmarinus

These pretty little evergreens have fragrant foliage and varied habits that make them worth growing in a container near your kitchen. Rosemary is a necessity in a Mediterranean-themed garden.

Growing
Rosemary prefers **full sun** but tolerates partial shade. The potting mix should be evenly **moist** and **well drained**; this plant doesn't like wet soil, but it doesn't like to dry out completely either. Rosemary is a tough plant that will survive almost anything but poor drainage. Fertilize no more than once a month during the growing season with quarter-strength fertilizer. In areas that receive frost, this tender shrub must be moved indoors in winter and kept in the brightest location available. Elsewhere, it is evergreen.

Tips
Rosemary can be grown in a container as a specimen or with other plants. Low-growing, spreading plants can be grown in hanging baskets. Rosemary can be clipped into balls or cone shapes and grown in an urn-type container for a formal, classic look.

Recommended
R. officinalis is a dense, bushy, evergreen shrub with narrow, dark green leaves. The habit varies somewhat among cultivars from strongly upright to prostrate and spreading. Flowers are usually in shades of blue, but pink-flowered cultivars are available.

R. officinalis 'Prostratus'

To keep plants bushy, pinch the tips back. The bits you pinch off can be used to flavor roast chicken, soups and stews.

Features: evergreen shrub; attractive, fragrant foliage; bright blue, sometimes pink, summer flowers **Height:** 8"–4' **Spread:** 1–4' **Hardiness:** zones 8–10; can be overwintered indoors

Rush

Juncus

J. effusus 'Spiralis' with impatiens

Rushes are popular, eye-catching plants, particularly the curly- or spiral-leaved cultivars, which prove fascinating to gardeners and visitors alike.

Growing

Rushes grow well in **full sun** or **partial shade**. The potting mix should be **acidic** and **moist to wet**. Fertilize no more than monthly during the growing season with quarter-strength fertilizer. In winter, move containers to a sheltered location protected from temperature fluctuations where plants are hardy. Grow them as annuals where they aren't hardy.

Tips

Plant rushes in moist containers with other water-loving plants such as iris and sedge. They can even be grown in shallow, gravel-filled water dishes, where they can be used to create a unique, living centerpiece for your patio table.

Recommended

J. effusus (soft rush) forms a tufted clump of long, flexible, stem-like leaves and bears insignificant flowers in summer. The species is rarely grown. **'Spiralis'** (corkscrew rush) forms a tangled mass of curling and corkscrew-like leaves, and cultivars with more corkscrew-like leaves are becoming available. **'Variegated Spiral Rush'** has white-streaked leaves. (Zones 6–8)

J. inflexus (hard rush) forms a clump of stiff, stem-like leaves. **'Afro'** has more tightly spiraled stems than 'Spiralis.'

Features: marginally aquatic perennial; decorative, stem-like leaves **Height:** 18–24" **Spread:** 12" **Hardiness:** zones 4–8

Salvia
Salvia

Proven Winners Selection *S. officinalis* 'Purpurea' with African daisy, sedge and others

Spikes of pretty flowers and attractive mounds of foliage help these plants blend into mixed containers.

Growing

Salvias grow best in **full sun** but tolerate light shade. The potting mix should be **humus rich, moist** and **well drained**. Some varieties take less water once established. Fertilize every two weeks during the growing season with quarter- to half-strength fertilizer. In cold winter areas, move containers to a sheltered location protected from temperature fluctuations in winter. Salvias are often treated like annuals where they won't survive winter.

Also called: sage **Features:** bushy habit; decorative, sometimes fragrant foliage; red, blue, purple, burgundy, lavender, plum, pink, orange, salmon, yellow, cream, white or bicolored, summer flowers **Height:** 12–24" **Spread:** 8–24" **Hardiness:** zones 4–10; tender perennial grown as an annual

S. splendens 'Sizzler White' with basil (above)
S. officinalis 'Icterina' (below)

Tips

Salvias are attractive plants that combine well with a wide variety of other plants and with each other. Use common sage with other edible herbs such as rosemary, basil and thyme for a fragrant, edible container. Place the fragrant variety where people can brush against it to release the spicy scent.

Recommended

S. farinacea (blue sage, mealy cup sage) has bright blue flowers clustered along stems powdered with silver. **'Victoria'** is a popular cultivar with silvery foliage and deep blue flowers. (Zones 8–10)

S. greggii (autumn sage) is a compact, shrubby perennial. It bears red, pink, purple or yellow flowers. **'Raspberry Royale'** bears raspberry red flowers. (Zones 7–9)

S. leucantha **'Santa Barbara,'** a Proven Selection from Proven Winners, is a compact (16–24" tall) version of the popular Mexican sage.

S. officinalis is a woody, mounding plant with soft, gray-green leaves. It bears light purple flowers in early and midsummer. Many attractive cultivars are available, including the silver-leaved **'Berggarten,'** the purple-leaved **'Purpurea,'** the yellow-margined **'Icterina'** and the green and cream variegated **'Tricolor,'** which has a pink flush to the new growth. (Zones 4–8)

S. splendens (salvia, scarlet sage) is a bushy perennial grown as an annual. It bears bright red flowers. Recently, cultivars have become available in white, pink, purple or orange. **'Salsa'** bears solid and bicolored flowers in shades of red, orange, purple, burgundy, cream or pink. **Sizzler Series** bears flowers in burgundy, lavender, pink, plum, red, salmon or white and salmon bicolored.

Scarlet Runner Bean

Phaseolus

Beautiful plants that also provide tasty vegetables are always a welcome addition to the container garden.

Growing

Scarlet runner beans grow best in **full sun**. The potting mix should be **moist** and **well drained**. Fertilize monthly with quarter- to half-strength fertilizer. These beans should be placed near something they can twine around. A porch railing or obelisk is suitable.

Tips

Scarlet runner beans have a carefree habit, twisting and twining around each other and any structure you can provide for them. They are delightful when grown in a container with an obelisk-type frame to climb. Create a similar look simply by poking three or four long poles into the container and tying them together at the top. Plant these beans in a hanging basket for a unique display.

Recommended

P. coccineus is a twining, annual vine. Scarlet red flowers are borne in clusters in summer, followed by long, edible pods. The edible, dark green pods are tender when young and are best eaten before they become stringy and tough. **Var. *alba*** (Dutch runner bean) bears white flowers. **'Painted Lady'** bears red and white bicolored flowers.

P. coccineus

If you have tall potted lilies, seed scarlet runner bean in the same pot. Once the lilies are done blooming, the tall stems can provide support for the bean as it makes its run upward.

Features: twining vine; red, white or bicolored, summer flowers; edible fruit **Height:** 6–8' **Spread:** 1–6' **Hardiness:** annual

Sedge
Carex

C. buchananii, from Proven Winners, with argyranthemum and others

With its green, blue, rust, bronze or gold foliage, sedge allows the gardener to add broad, colorful strokes or bright accents to the landscape.

Growing
Sedges grow well in **full sun** or **partial shade**. The potting mix should be neu-tral to **slightly alkaline** and **moist to wet**. 'Frosted Curls' is more drought tolerant than other sedges. A cool-season grass, it grows fastest in spring before slowing down when the temperatures rise. Fertilize every two weeks during the growing season with quarter-strength fertilizer. In cold areas, move containers to an unheated shed or garage where they will be protected from temperature fluctuations in winter, or grow them as annuals.

Features: tuft-forming, attractive habit; interesting, colorful foliage **Height:** 1–4' **Spread:** 1–4' **Hardiness:** zones 5–9

Tips

Sedges offer colorful foliage and rustic texture to contrast with other moisture-loving plants. The cascading habit of many of these grass-like plants makes them an interesting choice to grow as specimens in containers. Cut sedges back in early spring but after any snow is gone. Trimming too severely can be harmful—leave about one-third in place. Space them evenly around your patio or terrace for a formal display. 'Frosted Curls' contrasts well with coarse-textured plants.

Recommended

C. buchananii (leatherleaf sedge) forms a dense clump or tuft of narrow, arching, orange-brown leaves. (Zones 6–9)

C. comans **'Frosted Curls'** (New Zealand hair sedge) is a compact, clump-forming, evergreen perennial with fine-textured, pale green, weeping foliage. The foliage appears almost iridescent, with unusual curled and twisted tips. (Zones 7–9)

C. elata **'Aurea'** (Bowles' golden sedge) forms a clump of arching, grass-like, yellow leaves with green edges. It bears spikes of tiny, brown or green flowers in early summer.

C. flagellifera **'Toffee Twist Sedge'** has bronze, slender leaves with an attractive arching habit and grows 18–24" tall.

C. morrowii **'Aureovariegata'** (variegated Japanese sedge) forms low tufts of drooping, green-and-yellow-striped foliage. (Zones 6–9)

C. pendula (drooping sedge, weeping sedge) forms a clump of graceful, arching, grass-like, green leaves. Drooping spikes of brown flowers are borne on long stems in late spring and early summer.

C. flagellifera TOFFEE TWIST, a Proven Winners Selection, with petunia, sweet flag and argyranthemum (above), *C. comans* 'Frosted Curls' (below)

Sedum

Sedum

Sedum with sea lavender

Many sedums are grown for their foliage, which can range in color from steel gray-blue and green to red and burgundy. The flowers are an added bonus.

Also called: stonecrop **Features:** mat-forming or upright perennial; decorative, fleshy foliage; yellow, white, red or pink, summer to fall flowers **Height:** 2–24" **Spread:** 12–24" **Hardiness:** zones 3–9

Growing

Sedums prefer **full sun** but tolerate partial shade. The potting mix should be **neutral to alkaline** and **very well drained**. Where rain is plentiful, add perlite or sand to the potting soil and elevate the pots slightly by sitting them on pot feet. Fertilize no more than once a month during the growing season with half-strength fertilizer. In cold areas, move containers to a sheltered location protected from temperature fluctuations in winter.

Tips

Low-growing sedums make wonderful filler plants for mixed containers, where many of them will grow over the edge of the pot. Taller selections make good contrast plants for mixed containers.

Recommended

S. acre (gold moss stonecrop) is a low-growing, wide-spreading plant that bears small, yellow-green flowers.

S. **'Autumn Joy'** is a popular upright hybrid. The flowers open pink or red and later fade to deep bronze.

S. **'Fine Gold Leaf'** has miniature bright gold leaves that gather in tiny clumps.

S. rupestre **'Lemon Coral'** from Proven Winners features eye-catching spikes of yellow-green foliage with needle-shaped leaves.

S. spectabile (showy stonecrop) is an upright species with pink flowers. Cultivars are available.

S. spurium (two-row stonecrop) forms a low, wide mat of foliage with deep pink or white flowers. Many cultivars are available and are often grown for their colorful foliage.

Serviceberry
Amelanchier

The *Amelanchier* species are first-rate North American natives, bearing lacy, white flowers in spring, followed by edible berries. In fall, the foliage color ranges from glowing apricot to deep red.

Growing

Serviceberries grow well in **full sun** or **light shade**. The potting mix should be **acidic, humus rich, moist** and **well drained**. Fertilize every two weeks during the growing season with quarter-strength fertilizer. Move containers to a sheltered location protected from temperature fluctuations in winter.

Tips

With spring flowers, edible fruit, attractive leaves that turn red in fall and often artistic branch growth, serviceberries make beautiful specimen plants or even small shade trees for large containers.

Recommended

A. alnifolia (Pacific serviceberry) is a large, rounded, suckering, native shrub that bears clusters of white flowers in late spring and edible, dark purple fruit in summer. Shades of yellow, orange and red color the fall foliage. 'Regent' is a compact selection that grows 4–6' tall and wide.

A. canadensis (shadblow serviceberry) is a large, upright, suckering shrub. White, spring flowers are followed by edible, purple, summer fruit. The leaves turn orange, scarlet or red in fall.

A. canadensis

Serviceberry fruit can be used in place of blueberries in any recipe, having a similar but generally sweeter flavor.

Also called: saskatoon, juneberry, billberry **Features:** single- or multi-stemmed, deciduous large shrub or small tree; spring or early-summer flowers; edible fruit; fall color; habit; bark **Height:** 4–15' **Spread:** 4–15' **Hardiness:** zones 3–9

Snapdragon
Antirrhinum

A. majus cultivar

Features: clump-forming habit; glossy, green through bronze foliage; white, cream, yellow, orange, red, maroon, pink, purple or bicolored, summer flowers **Height:** 6"–4' **Spread:** 6–12" **Hardiness:** tender perennial grown as an annual

$\mathcal{G}$ardeners of all ages love the magic of these flowers, which look like delightful, tiny dragon heads.

Growing

Snapdragons prefer **full sun** but tolerate light shade or partial shade. The potting mix should be **humus rich, neutral to alkaline** and **well drained**. Fertilize every two weeks with quarter- to half-strength fertilizer. To encourage bushier growth, pinch the tips of young plants. Cut off the flower spikes as they fade to promote further blooming. Avoid overhead watering to reduce rust.

Tips

Snapdragons are bushy plants of variable height that look lovely planted alone or in mixed containers. There is even a trailing variety that does well in hanging baskets. The strong, upright, vividly colored flower spikes contrast beautifully with arching grasses and broad, leafy plants.

Recommended

A. majus is a bushy, clump-forming plant from which flower spikes emerge in summer. Many cultivars are available in dwarf (up to 12" tall), medium (12–24" tall) and giant (up to 4' tall) sizes. **'Floral Showers'** grows 6–8" tall and bears flowers in a wide range of solid colors and bicolors. **'Black Prince'** grows 18" tall and bears striking, dark purple-red flowers set against bronzy green foliage. **'Lampion'** has a trailing habit and cascades up to 36", making it a great plant for hanging baskets. **Rocket Series** cultivars have good heat tolerance, grow to 4' tall and produce long spikes of brightly colored flowers in many shades.

A. *majus* cultivar (above & below)

Snapdragons are interesting and long-lasting in fresh flower arrangements. The buds continue to mature and open long after the spike has been cut.

The genus name Antirrhinum *comes from the Greek language.* Anti *means "against" and* rhis *translates as "snout," referring to the shape of the flower.*

Snow-in-Summer
Cerastium

C. tomentosum

This Mediterranean native looks lovely spilling over the edge of a decorative terra-cotta container.

Snow-in-summer is a tough-as-nails plant that thrives even when neglected.

Growing
Snow-in-summer grows well in **full sun** or **partial shade**. The potting mix should be **well drained**. Fertilize no more than monthly during the growing season with quarter-strength fertilizer. Trim plants back after flowering is complete to encourage new growth and to keep plants looking tidy. Snow-in-summer will suffer in humid heat and in poorly drained soils. Move containers to a sheltered location protected from temperature fluctuations in winter.

Tips
Many gardeners have shied away from this potentially invasive plant, but it is this very quality that makes it a great container plant. It can only spread as far as the pot allows, and it is hardy and attractive. In a mixed container, be sure to use it with other vigorous plants. It makes a good choice for planting beneath a shrub or tree in a large container. Pair it with some dark-leaved sedums, and you'll have a mixed container planting that won't miss your watering can if you go on vacation.

Recommended
C. tomentosum forms a low mat of silvery gray foliage and bears white flowers in late spring.

Features: low, spreading perennial; silvery foliage; white, late-spring flowers **Height:** 2–12" **Spread:** 36" or more **Hardiness:** zones 1–8

Spider Plant
Chlorophytum

The grass-like, narrow leaf blades arch gracefully as they grow. The long, trailing stems cascade over the pot's edge and carry small plantlets that resemble baby spiders dangling from a silky thread.

Growing

Spider plants grow best in **light shade** or **partial shade** with protection from the hot afternoon sun. The potting mix should be **moist** and **well drained**. Plants are fairly drought tolerant. Fertilize every two weeks during the growing season with quarter-strength fertilizer. Plants can be moved indoors in winter, but it is often easier to snip off a few of the baby plantlets to grow over winter for use the following spring.

Tips

Spider plants make good filler plants for mixed containers. They grow quickly and produce flowers and stems of little plantlets while still quite young. The green or variegated leaves will brighten up a container shared with darker-leaved plants.

Recommended

C. comosum forms a clump of graceful, arching, grass-like leaves. Flowering stems emerge from the rosette bearing tiny, white flowers and young plantlets. The stems are pendant, weighed down by the plantlets. **'Milky Way'** has creamy leaf margins. **'Variegatum'** has cream to white leaf margins. **'Vittatum'** has leaves with a white central stripe and green margins.

C. comosum and *C. comosum* 'Vittatum'

Spider plants are incredibly adaptable, tolerating a wide range of conditions including heat or cold, sun or shade and humid or dry air. They are a good choice for balconies and roof gardens because they can handle the wind.

Features: clump-forming habit; decorative, arching, strap-like foliage; stems of trailing or dangling plantlets **Height:** 12" **Spread:** 24–36" **Hardiness:** tender perennial grown as an annual or overwintered indoors

Spruce
Picea

P. glauca var. *albertiana* 'Conica'

Spruces frequently produce branch mutations, and it is often from these that the dwarf selections are developed.

Features: conical or columnar, evergreen tree or shrub; attractive foliage; varied habit
Height: 2–6' **Spread:** 2–4' **Hardiness:** zones 2–8

With a varied selection of small spruces available in a variety of intriguing habits, they are worthy evergreens for the container garden.

Growing
Spruce trees grow best in **full sun**. The potting mix should be **neutral to acidic, moist** and **well drained**. Plant them in the biggest container you can so they won't tip over. Fertilize monthly during the growing season with quarter-strength fertilizer. Spray plants with a strong jet of water to keep them free of spider mites, especially in hot summer areas. Move containers to a sheltered location protected from the sun and wind in winter. They should be moved into the garden after three to five years.

Tips
Dwarf and slow-growing spruce cultivars are used as specimens in containers. Plant them with drought-tolerant plants in mixed containers because spruces will quickly consume the available moisture.

Recommended
P. abies (Norway spruce) has many dwarf cultivars. **'Little Gem'** is a slow-growing, rounded cultivar. **'Nidiformis'** (nest spruce) is a slow-growing, low, compact, mounding plant. **Forma *pendula*** are variable, weeping or prostrate forms of spruce. Staked at about 4', they develop into beautiful weeping specimens.

P. glauca var. *albertiana* 'Conica' (dwarf Alberta spruce) is a slow-growing, dense, conical, bushy shrub. Its needles may scorch in too windy or hot a location. **'Jean's Dilly'** is a smaller selection with shorter, thinner needles and twisted branch ends.

Swan River Daisy
Brachyscome (Brachycome)

B. iberidifolia BLUE ZEPHYR

This plant's dainty, daisy-like flowers and lacy, fern-like foliage make a winning combination.

Growing

Swan River daisy prefers **full sun** but benefits from light shade in the afternoon. The potting mix should be **well drained**. Allow the soil to dry between waterings. Fertilize once a month with half-strength fertilizer. Plant out early because cool spring weather encourages compact, sturdy growth. This plant tends to die back when summer gets too hot. If it begins to fade, cut it back and move it to a slightly shadier spot.

Tips

This versatile plant works well in mixed containers and hanging baskets. Plant it near the edges so that the bushy growth will hang out over the sides of the pot and the little flowers will poke through the leaves of its neighbors.

Recommended

B. iberidifolia bears blue-purple or pink-purple, daisy-like flowers all summer. BLUE ZEPHYR, a Proven Selection from Proven Winners, is a heat-tolerant cultivar that will bloom all season. 'Hot Candy' bears heat-tolerant, dark pink flowers that fade to pale pink.

Deadhead often, and remember to cut off the stem as well as the spent flower.

Features: bushy, mounding or spreading habit; blue, pink, white or purple, summer flowers, usually with yellow centers; feathery foliage **Height:** 6–18" **Spread:** 8–24" **Hardiness:** frost-tolerant annual

Sweet Alyssum
Lobularia

L. maritima with pineapple lily

Leave sweet alyssum out all winter. In spring, remove the previous year's growth to expose the self-sown seedlings below.

Features: fragrant flowers in pink, purple, yellow, salmon or white **Height:** 3–12" **Spread:** 6–24" **Hardiness:** annual

Sweet alyssum is an excellent plant for softening the edges of container plantings and should not be ignored when planting a fragrance garden. Just a few plants are enough to fill your garden with their sweet, honey-like fragrance.

Growing
Sweet alyssum prefers **full sun** but tolerates light shade. The potting mix should be **well drained** and **moist**. Fertilize monthly with quarter- to half-strength fertilizer. Sweet alyssum may die back a bit during hot and humid summers. Trim it back and ensure the potting mix remains moist to encourage new growth and more flowers when the weather cools.

Tips
Sweet alyssum is good for filling in spaces between taller plants in mixed containers. It will self-seed, sometimes quite a bit, and you may have seedlings popping up in other containers and odd areas in your garden and landscape.

Recommended
L. maritima forms a low, spreading mound of foliage. The entire plant appears to be covered in tiny blossoms when in full flower. Cultivars are available in a range of flower colors. The white varieties are the most fragrant.

Sweet Flag
Acorus

Sweet flags have glossy, often striped leaves that create an attractive display in a mixed container of moisture-loving plants.

Growing
Sweet flags grow best in **full sun**. The potting mix should be **moist to wet**. Fertilize monthly during the growing season with quarter- to half-strength fertilizer. Move containers to a sheltered location such as an unheated shed or garage in winter.

Tips
These plants are much admired for their habit as well as for the wonderful, spicy fragrance of the crushed leaves. Include sweet flags in a mixed container with plants such as calla lilies and elephant ears for a texturally intriguing, moisture-loving container.

Recommended
A. calamus (sweet flag) is a large, clump-forming plant with long, narrow, bright green, fragrant foliage. **'Variegatus'** has vertically striped yellow, cream and green leaves.

A. gramineus (dwarf sweet flag, Japanese rush) forms low, fan-shaped clumps of fragrant, glossy, green, narrow leaves. **'Minimus Aureus'** is a very low-growing cultivar with bright golden yellow leaves. **'Ogon,'** a Proven Selection from Proven Winners, has cream-and-green-striped leaves. **'Pusillus'** (dwarf Japanese rush) is a very low-growing cultivar. (Zones 5–11)

A. gramineus 'Ogon'

Sweet flag was a popular moat-side plant in the past.

Features: clump-forming perennial; narrow, stiff or arching, grass-like, sometimes variegated leaves; moisture loving **Height:** 4"–5'
Spread: 4–24" **Hardiness:** zones 4–11

Sweet Potato Vine
Ipomoea

I. batatas BLACK HEART, from Proven Winners

*The morning glories listed here are not related to the noxious weed called morning glory (*Convolvulus arvensis*) and will not persist in the garden.*

Features: twining climber; white, blue, pink or purple flowers; sometimes variegated or colorful foliage **Height:** 1–10' **Spread:** 12–24" **Hardiness:** annual; tender perennial grown as an annual

This genus offers vigorous vines that look stunning spilling over the edges of mixed containers. In addition to the ivy-leafed trailing sweet potato vine, it includes morning glory and moonflower.

Growing
All *Ipomoea* species grow well in **full sun**. The potting mix should be **light** and **well drained**. Fertilize sweet potato vine once a month with quarter- to half-

strength fertilizer. Other ipomoeas will bloom poorly if over-fertilized.

Tips

Sweet potato vines make excellent filler and accent plants in planters and hanging baskets. Sweet potato vines have colorful foliage, and morning glories and moonflowers have lovely, trumpet-shaped flowers. The climbing vines will grow up small trellises or other structures. Grow moonflower on a porch or on a trellis near a patio that is used in the evenings so that the sweetly scented flowers can be fully enjoyed.

Recommended

I. alba (moonflower) is a twining, perennial climber with heart-shaped leaves and sweetly scented, white flowers that open only at night.

I. batatas (sweet potato vine) is a twining, perennial climber that is usually treated as a bushy or trailing plant rather than a climber. It is grown for its attractive foliage rather than its flowers. Cultivars with different foliage color variations are available. BLACK HEART, a Proven Selection by Proven Winners, has heart-shaped, dark purple foliage. 'Blackie' has dark purple (almost black), deeply lobed leaves. 'Margarita' has yellow-green foliage on a fairly compact plant. 'Tricolor' is a compact plant with light green, cream and bright pink variegated leaves.

I. purpurea (morning glory) is a twining, annual climber with heart-shaped leaves and trumpet-shaped, purple, pink, blue or white flowers.

I. tricolor (morning glory) is a twining, annual climber with heart-shaped, purple or blue flowers with white throats. There are several cultivars, including the popular 'Heavenly Blue,' which has sky blue flowers with white centers.

I. batatas 'Margarita' with coleus, English ivy, lamium and others (above), *I. batatas* 'Margarita' with juniper, coral bells and bamboo grass (below)

Thyme
Thymus

T. x citriodorus 'Golden King' with parsley, rosemary and others

In the Middle Ages, it was believed that drinking a thyme infusion would enable one to see fairies.

Features: mounding or creeping perennial; purple, pink or white, late-spring to early-summer flowers; tiny, fuzzy or glossy, often fragrant foliage **Height:** 2–18" **Spread:** 4–16" **Hardiness:** zones 3–9

Upright or creeping, thyme is an excellent plant for a container. Its tiny flowers attract a variety of pollinators. The leaves are pleasantly aromatic.

Growing

Thyme grows in **full sun** to light shade. The potting mix should be **humus rich** and **very well drained**. Mix in compost or earthworm castings. Keep the soil relatively dry. These plants are fairly drought tolerant. Move containers to a sheltered location protected from temperature fluctuations in winter.

Tips

Thyme is a nice addition to your herb collection, growing nicely by itself or mixed with other herbs. It can also be used at the edge of a mixed container, where the tiny leaves will soften the appearance of coarser-leaved companions.

Recommended

T. citriodorus (lemon-scented thyme) forms a tidy, rounded mound of lemon-scented foliage and pale pink flowers. **'Argenteus'** has silver-edged leaves. **'Golden King'** has yellow-margined leaves. (Zones 5–9)

T. serpyllum (mother of thyme, wild thyme) is a low, creeping, mat-forming plant. It bears purple flowers. **'Elfin'** forms tiny, dense mounds of foliage. It rarely flowers. **'Minimalist'** ('Minimus') is lower growing than the species and bears pink flowers. **'Snowdrift'** has white flowers.

T. vulgaris (common thyme) forms a bushy mound of dark green leaves. The flowers may be purple, pink or white. **'Silver Posie'** has pale pink flowers and silver-edged leaves. (Zones 4–9)

Tradescantia

Tradescantia

*O*ften reserved for hanging baskets, these plants create a stunning display of arching foliage that looks lovely in a tall, urn-shaped planter.

Growing

Tradescantias grow well in **partial shade** or strong light but keep them out of direct sun. The potting mix should be **moist** and **well drained**. Fertilize every two weeks during the growing season with quarter- to half-strength fertilizer. Move containers to a sheltered location protected from temperature fluctuations in winter. Tender plants will have to be brought indoors before the first frost or replaced the following summer.

Tips

Tradescantias make good hanging-basket plants and can be grown alone or with other trailing plants. In containers, they make attractive companions for coarse-textured and upright-growing plants.

Recommended

T. andersoniana (spiderwort) forms a clump of stems and arching, strap-like foliage. Clusters of blue, purple, pink, red or white flowers are produced from early summer to fall. **'Concord Grape'** has silvery blue-green foliage and dark purple flowers. **'Little Doll'** is a dwarf selection that bears light blue flowers.

T. pallida **'Purpurea'** ('Purple Heart') is a tender, trailing or mound-forming plant with purple stems and bronzy purple leaves. It bears pink flowers in summer. This plant tolerates drought.

T. x *andersoniana* cultivar with golden hakone grass, begonia, hosta and others (above), *T.* x *andersoniana* 'Sweet Kate' from Proven Winners (below)

Also called: wandering Jew, inch plant **Features:** clump-forming, mound-forming or trailing habit; colorful foliage; attractive pink, blue, purple, red or white, summer flowers **Height:** 8–24" **Spread:** 12–24" **Hardiness:** zones 3–9; tender perennial grown as an annual

Tulip
Tulipa

T. hybrid

Tulips are a welcome sight as we enjoy the warm days of spring. Tulips perform best in cooler areas.

Growing

Tulips grow best in **full sun,** but shorter tulip varieties, such as *T. fosteriana,* and the rock garden tulips do best in pots that don't get full sun. The potting mix should be **well drained**. Plant bulbs in fall and keep containers in a **sheltered** location. In spring, plant bulbs that have been cold treated. Fertilize with quarter-strength fertilizer every two weeks as flowering finishes and until the foliage begins to fade if you are planning to keep your bulbs for fall planting or storing over winter.

When your tulips are done blooming, dig them from the pot and add summer annuals, or just cut them to the ground and plant right on top of the bulbs. Tulips don't bloom as well the second year in pots, so treat them as annuals or replant them into the ground after they bloom the first year.

To grow tulips in warmer areas, refrigerate bulbs in a paper bag for six weeks before planting in January. Drop some low-nitrogen fertilizer in the planting hole. Water thoroughly immediately after planting, then sparingly until leaves emerge. After that, provide regular water.

Tips

Tulips provide the best display when planted in groups.

Recommended

There are about 100 species and thousands of hybrids and cultivars. They come in dozens of shades except blue, with many bicolored and multi-colored varieties. Check with your garden center in early fall for the best selection.

Features: perennial bulb; spring flowers
Height: 6–30" **Spread:** 2–8" **Hardiness:** zones 3–8

Verbena
Verbena

Verbena is an outstanding container and hanging-basket plant. The trailing stems poke brightly colored flower clusters out in unexpected places.

Growing

Verbenas grow best in **full sun**. The potting mix should be **very well drained**. Water consistently and do not allow them to dry out. Fertilize every two weeks in summer with half-strength fertilizer. Pinch young plants back to encourage bushy growth. Verbenas will overwinter in containers in mild areas.

Tips

Use verbenas in mixed containers, hanging baskets and window boxes. They are good substitutes for ivy geraniums where the sun is hot and where a roof overhang keeps these mildew-prone plants dry. Verbena mixes well with a variety of other plants including million bells, lantana, nemesia, petunia and gaura.

Recommended

V. x *hybrida* is a bushy plant that may be upright or spreading. It bears clusters of small flowers in shades of white, purple, blue, pink, red, salmon, coral or yellow. **Babylon Series** is a group of compact, bushy plants with flowers in shades of deep or light blue, bright or light pink, dark or light purple, red or white. **'Peaches and Cream'** is a spreading plant with flowers that open soft peachy pink and fade to white. SUPERBENA SERIES from Proven Winners is a group of mounding then cascading, mildew-resistant plants with large, vividly colored flowers in shades of purple, burgundy, coral, red, pink or blue.

V. SUPERBENA DARK BLUE with salvia and euphorbia

To rejuvenate foliage and encourage more blooms, cut back the plants by half in midsummer.

Features: mounding to cascading habit; flowers in shades of red, pink, purple, blue or white, sometimes with white centers **Height:** 8–24" **Spread:** 12–24" **Hardiness:** tender perennial grown as an annual

Vinca
Vinca

V. minor and *V. minor* 'Illumination' with geraniums

With glossy, deep green leaves and periwinkle blue flowers, vinca has an attractive presence in the container garden. This evergreen plant will provide you with color during the chilly, gray days of winter.

Growing
Grow vinca in **partial to full shade**. The potting mix should be evenly **moist** and **well drained**. Fertilize monthly during the growing season with quarter-strength fertilizer. Move containers to a sheltered location out of the wind in winter.

Tips
Vinca is a useful, attractive filler plant for containers and hanging baskets. Poke a few rooted stems in here and there to provide a dark green background in your mixed containers.

Recommended
V. major (greater periwinkle) forms a low mat of trailing stems with glossy, dark green leaves. It bears purple or blue flowers from spring to fall. It is often grown as an annual. **'Variegata'** has irregular, creamy margins on light green, glossy leaves. (Zones 7–11)

V. minor (lesser periwinkle) forms a low, loose mat of trailing stems. Purple or blue flowers are borne in spring and sporadically all summer. **'Atropurpurea'** bears reddish purple flowers. **'Illumination'** has vivid gold foliage marked with green patches.

Also called: periwinkle **Features:** low, trailing, hardy or tender vine; green or variegated, glossy foliage; blue-purple, pale blue, reddish purple or white, mid-spring to fall flowers **Height:** 4–12" **Spread:** 2–4' **Hardiness:** zones 4–11

Weigela
Weigela

Weigelas have been improved through breeding, and specimens with more compact forms, longer flowering periods and greater cold tolerance are now available. These fragrant plants attract hummingbirds and butterflies.

Growing

Weigelas prefer **full sun** but tolerate partial shade. The potting mix should be **well drained**. Fertilize monthly during the growing season with half-strength fertilizer. To promote flowering, cut spent branches back to unflowered side branches. In areas that receive frost, move containers to a sheltered location protected from temperature fluctuations in winter.

Tips

With their attractive foliage and long flowering period, weigelas are great as focal points alone or in mixed containers. Combine a purple-leaved weigela with a silver-leaved, white-flowered, trailing plant such as snow-in-summer to soften the edges of the container and to create a lovely contrast.

Recommended

W. florida is a bushy, spreading shrub with arching branches that bears clusters of dark pink flowers. Many hybrids and cultivars are available. CARNAVAL bears red, white or pink flowers. **'Eye-catcher'** from Proven Winners was named one of the best 18 trees and shrubs for 2008 by *Better Homes and Gardens* and has variegated foliage and dark red flowes. **'Polka'** has bright pink flowers. **'Red Prince'** produces dark red flowers. **'Rubidor'** has yellow foliage and red flowers. **'Variegata'** has yellow and

W. florida FINE WINE, a Proven Winners Color Choice Selection

green variegated foliage and pink flowers. WINE & ROSES has dark burgundy foliage and rosy pink flowers. FINE WINE is a compact selection of WINE & ROSES with good branching, dark burgundy foliage and hot pink flowers. MIDNIGHT WINE is a low, mounding dwarf with dark burgundy foliage.

Weigela will become too large for a container after three to five years and should be moved to the garden when it does.

Features: upright or low, spreading, deciduous shrub; green, bronze or purple foliage; attractive late-spring, early-summer and, sporadically, fall flowers **Height:** 1–6' **Spread:** 1–4' **Hardiness:** zones 3–8

Yarrow
Achillea

A. millefolium

Yarrow will happily self-seed, eventually turning up in most of your containers and anywhere else the seeds happen to land.

Features: clump-forming perennial; white, yellow, red, orange, pink or purple, midsummer to early-fall flowers; attractive foliage; spreading habit **Height:** 4"–4' **Spread:** 12–36" **Hardiness:** zones 2–8

arrows are informal, tough plants with a fantastic color range.

Growing
Yarrows grow best in **full sun**. The potting mix should be **light** and **well drained**. These plants tolerate drought. Fertilize no more than monthly during the growing season with quarter-strength fertilizer. Too much fertilizer results in weak, floppy growth. Deadhead to prolong blooming. In cold areas, move containers to a sheltered location protected from temperature fluctuations in winter.

Tips
Yarrow thrives in hot, dry locations where nothing else will grow. If you often forget to water, yarrow could be the plant for you. Combine it with other drought-tolerant plants such as sedum and hens and chicks. The fine, ferny foliage of yarrow will contrast with the coarse, fleshy foliage of the other two plants. In warm areas, all these plants perform better with some supplemental water.

Recommended
A. millefolium (common yarrow) forms a clump of soft, finely divided foliage and bears white flowers. Many cultivars exist, with flowers in a wide range of colors. '**Apple Blossom**' has light pink flowers. '**Paprika**' bears yellow-centered, red flowers that fade to pink, yellow or cream. '**Summer Pastels**' bears white, pink, yellow, purple and sometimes red or salmon-colored flowers. '**Terra Cotta**' has orange-red flowers that fade to light rusty orange or creamy orange.

Yew

Taxus

Yews are among the only reliable evergreens for full sun and deep shade.

Growing

Yews grow well in any light conditions from **full sun to full shade**. The potting mix should be **moist** and **well drained**. Fertilize monthly during the growing season with half-strength fertilizer. Move them to a sheltered location out of the wind and sun in winter.

Tips

Yews are often used to create topiary specimens and can be clipped to maintain a small, neat form for a container. Specimens can be planted alone or used with annuals and perennials for a mixed display.

Male and female flowers are borne on separate plants. Both must be present for the attractive red seed cups to form.

Recommended

T. x *media* (English-Japanese yew), a cross between *T. baccata* (English yew) and *T. cuspidata* (Japanese yew), has the vigor of English yew and the cold hardiness of Japanese yew. It forms a rounded, upright tree or shrub, though the size and form can vary among the many cultivars. **'Brownii'** is a dense, rounded cultivar. **'Hicksii'** is a narrow, columnar form. **'Tautonii'** is a slow-growing, rounded, spreading cultivar.

These trees tolerate windy, dry and polluted conditions but dislike excessive heat, and on the south or southwest side of a building, they may suffer needle scorch.

T. x *media* 'Sunburst' (above)
T. x *media* 'Densiformis' (below)

Features: conical, columnar, bushy or spreading, evergreen tree or shrub; attractive foliage; red fruit **Height:** 1–10' **Spread:** 1–5' **Hardiness:** zones 4–7

Yucca
Yucca

Yucca adds a bold presence and texture to your mixed planters.

Growing

Yucca grows best in **full sun** but tolerates partial shade. The potting mix must be **well drained**. This plant is very drought tolerant. Fertilize no more than once a month during the growing season with quarter-strength fertilizer. In cold weather areas, move it to a sheltered location in winter, or just leave it where it is. If it doesn't make it through winter, simply replace it in spring. Remove spent flower spikes and dead leaves as needed.

Tips

Yucca makes a strong architectural statement and is used as a specimen in planters to give a garden a southern appearance. Combine it with low, soft, trailing plants to create some contrast.

Yuccas are perfect for urns because many urn-shaped containers have so little room for soil that they dry out quickly. Yuccas also grow in a natural symmetrical shape, giving them a formal look for classic gardens. Because the leaves can be sharp, place the containers away from walkways.

Recommended

Y. filamentosa has long, stiff, finely serrated, pointed leaves with threads that peel back from the edges. It is the most frost-hardy species available. **'Bright Edge'** has leaves with yellow margins. **'Golden Sword'** has leaves with yellow centers and green margins. **'Hofer's Blue'** has attractive, blue-green leaves and tolerates salt.

Y. filamentosa with maidenhair vine, African daisy, vinca and dracaena

---

Also called: Adam's needle **Features:** stiff, rosette-forming, evergreen perennial; stiff, decorative foliage; white or creamy, summer flowers **Height:** 24–36"; up to 6' in flower **Spread:** 24–36" **Hardiness:** zones 5–10

Glossary

Acidic soil: soil with a pH lower than 7.0

Annual: a plant that germinates, flowers, sets seed and dies in one growing season

Alkaline soil: soil with a pH higher than 7.0

Basal foliage: leaves that form from the crown, at the base of the plant

Bract: a modified leaf at the base of a flower or flower cluster

Corm: a bulb-like, food-storing, underground stem, resembling a bulb without scales

Crown: the part of the plant at or just below soil level where the shoots join the roots

Cultivar: a cultivated plant variety with one or more distinct differences from the species, e.g., in flower color or disease resistance

Deadhead: to remove spent flowers to maintain a neat appearance and encourage a longer blooming season

Direct sow: to sow seeds directly in the garden

Dormancy: a period of plant inactivity, usually during winter or unfavorable conditions

Double flower: a flower with an unusually large number of petals

Espalier: a tree trained from a young age to grow on a single plane

Genus: a category of biological classification between the species and family levels; the first word in a scientific name indicates the genus

Grafting: a type of propagation in which a stem or bud of one plant is joined onto the rootstock of another plant of a closely related species

Hardy: capable of surviving cold weather or frost without protection

Hip: the fruit of a rose, containing the seeds

Humus: decomposed or decomposing organic material in the soil

Hybrid: a plant resulting from natural or human-induced cross-breeding between varieties, species or genera

Neutral soil: soil with a pH of 7.0

Offset: a horizontal branch that forms at the base of a plant and produces new plants from buds at its tips

Panicle: a compound flower structure with groups of flowers on short stalks

Perennial: a plant that takes three or more years to complete its life cycle

pH: a measure of acidity or alkalinity

Rhizome: a root-like, food-storing stem that grows horizontally at or just below soil level, from which new shoots may emerge

Rootball: the root mass and surrounding soil of a plant

Seedhead: dried, inedible fruit that contains seeds; the fruiting stage of the inflorescence

Self-seeding: reproducing by means of seeds without human assistance, so that new plants constantly replace those that die

Semi-double flower: a flower with petals in two or three rings

Single flower: a flower with a single ring of typically four or five petals

Species: the fundamental unit of biological classification; the entity from which cultivars and varieties are derived

Standard: a shrub or small tree grown with an erect main stem, accomplished either through pruning and training or by grafting the plant onto a tall, straight stock

Sucker: a shoot that comes up from the root, often some distance from the plant; it can be separated to form a new plant once it develops its own roots

Tender: incapable of surviving the climatic conditions of a given region and requiring protection from frost or cold

Tuber: the thick section of a rhizome bearing nodes and buds

Variegation: foliage that has more than one color, often patched or striped or bearing leaf margins of a different color

Variety: a naturally occurring variant of a species

SPECIES
by Common Name

Species by Common Name	Full Sun	Light Shade	Partial Shade	Full Shade	Soil-based	Soil-less	Variegated	Flowers	Foliage	Fruit/Seed	Scent	Specimen	Grouping
African Daisy	•					•		•					•
Agapanthus	•	•	•			•		•	•				•
Aloe	•	•	•	•		•	•	•	•				
Angelonia	•					•	•	•	•		•		
Angel's Trumpet	•					•		•	•		•	•	
Arborvitae	•	•	•		•	•	•		•			•	
Argyranthemum	•					•		•	•				•
Asparagus Fern		•	•			•			•				
Bacopa			•			•		•	•				
Basil	•					•			•		•		
Bay Laurel	•	•	•		•	•			•			•	
Begonia		•	•			•		•	•				•
Bidens	•					•		•	•				
Black-Eyed Susan	•		•			•		•					•
Black-Eyed Susan Vine	•	•	•			•		•	•				
Blood Grass	•		•			•			•				
Blue Fescue	•		•			•			•				
Blue Oat Grass	•					•			•				
Bougainvillea	•					•	•	•	•				
Bugleweed		•	•			•	•	•	•				
Calla Lily	•					•		•	•			•	
Canna Lily	•					•	•	•	•			•	
Catch-Fly	•	•				•		•					
Cilantro·Coriander	•					•		•	•	•			
Citrus	•				•	•		•	•	•	•	•	
Clematis	•					•		•	•				•
Cleome	•					•		•	•		•	•	
Clover	•		•			•	•	•	•				
Coleus		•	•			•	•		•				•
Coral Bells		•	•			•	•	•	•				•
Croscosmia	•					•		•	•			•	
Cuphea	•		•			•		•					
Dahlia	•					•		•	•			•	

SOIL CONDITION						FORM					SPECIES by Common Name
Moist	Well-drained	Dry	Fertile	Average	Poor	Upright	Bushy	Climber/Trailer	Architectural	Page Number	
•	•		•	•		•	•			52	African Daisy
•	•		•						•	53	Agapanthus
	•			•		•				54	Aloe
•	•			•		•				55	Angelonia
•	•		•	•		•	•		•	56	Angel's Trumpet
•	•			•	•	•	•			57	Arborvitae
	•			•			•			59	Argyranthemum
•				•			•	•		60	Asparagus Fern
•	•			•					•	61	Bacopa
•	•		•	•			•			62	Basil
•	•			•		•	•			63	Bay Laurel
	•		•	•			•	•		64	Begonia
•	•		•	•			•			66	Bidens
•	•	•		•		•				67	Black-Eyed Susan
•	•		•	•				•		69	Black-Eyed Susan Vine
•	•			•		•			•	70	Blood Grass
•	•			•					•	71	Blue Fescue
	•				•				•	72	Blue Oat Grass
•	•		•	•		•	•	•		73	Bougainvillea
	•			•			•	•		74	Bugleweed
•	•		•	•		•			•	75	Calla Lily
•	•		•	•		•			•	77	Canna Lily
•	•		•	•		•	•			78	Catch-Fly
	•			•		•				79	Cilantro·Coriander
	•			•		•	•			80	Citrus
•	•		•	•		•	•	•		81	Clematis
•	•			•	•	•	•			83	Cleome
•	•			•	•		•			84	Clover
•	•		•	•			•			85	Coleus
•	•			•			•			87	Coral Bells
•	•			•					•	89	Crocosmia
•	•			•		•	•			90	Cuphea
•	•		•	•		•	•			91	Dahlia

SPECIES
by Common Name

	LIGHT				SOIL MIX		FEATURES						
Species	Full Sun	Light Shade	Partial Shade	Full Shade	Soil-based	Soil-less	Variegated	Flowers	Foliage	Fruit/Seed	Scent	Specimen	Grouping
Daylily	•	•	•	•		•		•	•			•	•
Diascia	•		•			•		•	•				
Dogwood	•	•	•	•	•	•	•	•	•	•		•	
Dusty Miller	•								•				•
Dwarf Morning Glory	•					•		•					
Echeveria	•		•			•	•	•	•				
Elder	•		•		•	•	•	•	•	•		•	
Elephant Ears		•		•		•			•			•	
Euonymus	•				•	•	•		•			•	
Euphorbia	•	•				•		•	•			•	
False Cypress	•				•	•			•	•		•	
Fan Flower	•	•				•		•					
Flowering Maple	•	•				•	•	•	•			•	
Foamflower		•	•	•		•	•	•	•				•
Fothergilla	•	•	•		•	•		•	•			•	•
Fuchsia		•	•			•		•	•				
Gaura	•					•	•	•	•				
Geranium	•					•	•	•	•		•		•
Glory Bush	•					•		•	•			•	
Golden Hakone Grass		•	•			•	•		•				•
Golden Marguerite	•					•		•	•				•
Hardy Geranium		•	•			•		•	•				
Hebe	•		•		•	•		•	•			•	•
Heliotrope	•					•		•	•		•		
Hens and Chicks	•		•			•	•	•	•				•
Hosta		•	•				•	•	•		•		
Hydrangea	•		•		•	•		•	•			•	
Hyssop	•					•		•	•		•		
Impatiens		•	•			•		•					•
Iris	•					•	•	•	•				
Japanese Painted Fern		•	•	•		•	•		•				
Jasmine	•		•		•	•	•	•	•		•		
Kalanchoe		•	•			•		•	•				

| SOIL CONDITION | | | | | | FORM | | | | | SPECIES by Common Name |
Moist	Well-drained	Dry	Fertile	Average	Poor	Upright	Bushy	Climber/Trailer	Architectural	Page Number	
•	•			•					•	93	Daylily
•	•		•	•		•	•	•		94	Diascia
	•			•		•	•			95	Dogwood
	•			•	•		•			97	Dusty Miller
	•				•		•			98	Dwarf Morning Glory
	•			•						99	Echeveria
•	•			•		•	•			100	Elder
•				•		•			•	102	Elephant Ears
•	•			•			•	•		103	Euonymous
•	•				•		•			105	Euphorbia
•	•			•		•	•			107	False Cypress
•	•			•			•	•		109	Fan Flower
•	•		•	•		•				110	Flowering Maple
•	•			•			•			111	Foamflower
•	•			•			•			112	Fothergilla
•	•		•				•	•		113	Fuchsia
	•			•			•			115	Gaura
	•		•	•			•			116	Geranium
•	•		•	•			•			118	Glory Bush
•	•		•	•				•	•	119	Golden Hakone Grass
	•	•		•	•		•			120	Golden Marguerite
	•			•			•			121	Hardy Geranium
•	•			•			•			123	Hebe
•	•			•			•			125	Heliotrope
	•			•	•					126	Hens and Chicks
•	•			•			•			127	Hosta
•	•			•			•	•		129	Hydrangea
	•			•		•	•			131	Hyssop
•	•			•			•			132	Impatiens
•	•			•		•			•	133	Iris
•				•			•			135	Japanese Painted Fern
•	•			•			•	•		137	Jasmine
	•			•		•	•	•		138	Kalanchoe

SPECIES
by Common Name

Species	LIGHT				SOIL MIX		FEATURES						
	Full Sun	Light Shade	Partial Shade	Full Shade	Soil-based	Soil-less	Variegated	Flowers	Foliage	Fruit/Seed	Scent	Specimen	Grouping
Lady's Mantle		•	•			•		•	•				
Lamium		•	•			•	•	•	•				
Lantana	•					•		•	•				
Lavender	•					•		•	•		•		
Licorice Plant	•					•	•		•				
Lilac	•				•	•			•			•	•
Lilyturf		•	•			•	•	•	•				•
Lobelia	•		•			•		•					•
Lotus Vine	•		•			•			•				
Lungwort		•	•	•		•	•	•	•				
Lysimachia	•		•			•		•					
Maidenhair Fern		•	•			•			•				•
Mandevilla	•		•		•	•		•	•			•	
Maple	•	•			•	•			•			•	
Million Bells	•					•		•					
Mondo Grass	•	•	•			•		•	•				•
Monkey Flower		•	•			•		•					•
Nasturtium	•					•	•	•	•				
Nemesia	•					•		•					
Nicotiana	•	•	•			•		•	•		•		
Oregano	•					•			•		•		
Oxalis	•		•			•		•	•				
Pansy	•					•		•					•
Parsley	•		•			•			•				
Penstemon	•					•		•					
Perilla	•		•			•			•				
Petunia	•					•		•				•	•
Phlox	•					•		•			•		
Phormium	•					•	•		•			•	
Piggyback Plant		•	•	•		•	•		•			•	
Plectranthus		•	•			•	•		•				
Poor Man's Orchid	•		•			•		•					•
Purple Fountain Grass	•					•		•	•				

Moist	Well-drained	Dry	Fertile	Average	Poor	Upright	Bushy	Climber/Trailer	Architectural	Page Number	SPECIES by Common Name
•	•		•	•			•			139	Lady's Mantle
•	•			•	•			•		140	Lamium
•	•		•				•	•		142	Lantana
	•			•	•	•	•			143	Lavender
	•			•			•	•		144	Licorice Plant
	•			•	•	•	•			145	Lilac
•	•			•	•	•			•	147	Lilyturf
•	•			•		•	•	•		148	Lobelia
	•			•	•		•	•		150	Lotus Vine
•	•		•	•			•			151	Lungwort
•	•			•	•	•	•	•		152	Lysimachia
•	•			•	•		•			153	Maidenhair Fern
•	•		•	•			•	•		154	Mandevilla
	•			•	•	•	•			155	Maple
•	•		•	•			•	•		157	Million Bells
•	•			•					•	158	Mondo Grass
•				•	•		•	•		159	Monkey Flower
•	•			•	•		•	•		160	Nasturtium
•	•			•			•	•		161	Nemesia
•	•		•	•	•	•			•	162	Nicotiana
	•			•	•		•			163	Oregano
	•			•			•			164	Oxalis
•	•			•						165	Pansy
•	•			•			•			167	Parsley
	•	•		•	•	•	•			168	Penstemon
•	•		•				•			169	Perilla
	•			•	•		•	•		170	Petunia
•	•			•			•	•		172	Phlox
•	•			•		•			•	173	Phormium
•	•			•			•	•		174	Piggyback Plant
•	•			•			•	•		175	Plectranthus
•	•		•			•		•		176	Poor Man's Orchid
	•			•	•	•			•	177	Purple Fountain Grass

SPECIES
by Common Name

	LIGHT				SOIL MIX		FEATURES						
	Full Sun	Light Shade	Partial Shade	Full Shade	Soil-based	Soil-less	Variegated	Flowers	Foliage	Fruit/Seed	Scent	Specimen	Grouping
Rhododendron·Azalea		•	•		•	•		•	•			•	
Rose	•				•	•		•	•	•	•	•	
Rosemary	•					•		•	•		•	•	
Rush	•		•			•			•				
Salvia	•					•	•	•	•		•		
Scarlet Runner Bean	•					•		•	•	•			
Sedge	•		•			•			•			•	
Sedum	•					•		•	•				•
Serviceberry	•	•			•	•		•	•	•		•	
Snapdragon	•					•		•	•				•
Snow-in-Summer	•		•			•		•	•				•
Spider Plant		•	•		•	•	•		•				
Spruce	•				•	•			•	•		•	
Swan River Daisy	•					•		•	•				•
Sweet Alyssum	•					•			•		•		•
Sweet Flag	•					•	•		•				
Sweet Potato Vine	•					•	•	•	•				
Thyme	•					•	•	•	•		•		
Tradescantia	•		•			•		•	•				•
Tulip	•					•		•					•
Verbena	•					•		•					
Vinca		•	•	•		•	•	•	•				
Weigela	•				•	•	•	•	•			•	
Yarrow	•					•		•	•				
Yew	•	•	•	•	•	•			•	•		•	
Yucca	•					•	•		•			•	

Moist	Well-drained	Dry	Fertile	Average	Poor	Upright	Bushy	Climber/Trailer	Architectural	Page Number	SPECIES by Common Name
•	•		•				•			179	Rhododendron·Azalea
•	•		•	•			•			181	Rose
•	•			•	•	•	•	•		183	Rosemary
•				•	•				•	184	Rush
•	•			•			•			185	Salvia
•	•			•				•		187	Scarlet Runner Bean
•				•					•	188	Sedge
	•			•	•	•	•			190	Sedum
•	•			•		•	•			191	Serviceberry
	•		•	•		•	•			192	Snapdragon
	•			•	•					194	Snow-in-Summer
•	•			•			•	•		195	Spider Plant
•	•			•		•	•			196	Spruce
	•			•			•			197	Swan River Daisy
•	•			•			•			198	Sweet Alyssum
•				•		•			•	199	Sweet Flag
	•			•	•			•		200	Sweet Potato Vine
	•			•	•	•	•			202	Thyme
•	•			•			•	•		203	Tradescantia
	•			•		•				204	Tulip
	•		•	•			•	•		205	Verbena
•	•			•				•		206	Vinca
	•			•			•			207	Weigela
	•			•	•		•			208	Yarrow
•	•			•		•	•			209	Yew
	•	•	•	•	•	•			•	210	Yucca

Index of Recommended Plant Names

Main entries are in **boldface**; botanical names are in *italics*.

About the Authors

Freelance writer and Master Gardener Jennifer E. Beaver discovered a passion for plants after witnessing their transformative power in neighborhoods. She helped found a group that successfully saves urban landscape trees, thereby reducing pollution and preserving property values. Captivated by the delights of container gardening, she is always on the prowl for new plant combinations to fill re-purposed containers. Since moving to California, she continues to try to recreate the flavor of her father's Jersey tomatoes.

Don Williamson has turned his passion for gardening into his life's work. His background is in landscaping, golf course construction and management, and in the design and construction of formal landscape settings. With a degree in Applied Horticultural Technology and professional certificates in Turf Management, he has written and co-written several gardening books.

31901046619252